A Song Called Teaching

Ebbs and Flows of Experiential and Empathetic Pedagogies

A Song Called Teaching

Ebbs and Flows of Experiential and Empathetic Pedagogies

Edited by

Honey Oberoi Vahali

AAKAR

A Song Called Teaching: Ebbs and Flows of Experiential and Empathetic Pedagogies
Edited by Honey Oberoi Vahali

First Published 2019

ISBN 978-93-5002-590-1 (Hb)

Published by
AAKAR BOOKS
28 E Pocket IV, Mayur Vihar Phase I
Delhi 110 091
www.aakarbooks.com

Designed by
Limited Colors, Delhi 110 092

Printed at
Sapra Brothers, Noida

To our students
and also to all those young lives who could never
reach a university's threshold
and
to all teachers
who in spite of these difficult times
dare to believe in the classroom as a space of love

Contents

Section 5: Metamorphosing from a Caterpillar into a Butterfly

Section 6: Through the Rear View Mirror: Reminiscences of Teachers in Becoming

Foreword

A society that has lost its teachers is dead. No matter how much we celebrate technical efficiency and economic progress, a society needs great teachers to arrive at a higher stage of ethical, cultural and spiritual growth. Even though in this cynical/ pragmatic age, all great dreams and aspirations are devalued, there are silent *karmayogis* who keep doing things that arouse hope—the confidence in human potentialities. No wonder, when I read a book of this kind, it awakens my sensibilities, opens all the windows of my mind, and makes me realize that there are teachers who heed the call of the vocation and transform teaching into a sacred act of communion.

As a teacher, I find my soul in this book. Because I too believe that teaching is not merely an act of dissemination of expertized knowledge in the classroom; teaching is not just about completing the syllabus, conducting examinations and 'measuring' one's aptitude; teaching is not merely about producing specialists and technical professionals. Instead, the great act of teaching is a nuanced pedagogic art, a move towards a profound relationship filled with the ethic of care and empathy, a possibility of communicative interaction. I too realize the need for a community of learners 'not driven by competition but cooperation to work their way to a 'being mode' of life rather than the 'having mode' of life and existence'.

The readers need to understand the relevance of this book. This is possible if they can perceive the crisis confronting the domain of education. In this context, I wish to make three points. First, we find ourselves in a world in which the instrumental rationality of the market invades every sphere of life, and even education becomes a marketable product—yet, another instrument for promoting one-dimensional technocratic reasoning. With the blooming business of education shops and market-friendly courses like hotel management and fashion technology, a teacher becomes merely a 'service provider', and students are just consumers of 'skills'. In an environment of this kind, there is no ecstasy; there is no Paulo Freire or Rabindranath Tagore; there is only the business contract. In fact, it has 'obscured the imagination of education as a communion of minds and beings'. It is sad that 'the humane, unconscious, unknowable and emotive aspects of engaging with the self and the other have been relegated to the margin'. Second, we see yet another transformation—from a dialogic teacher to a tutor of a coaching centre assuring instant success. Bring the likes of Jiddu Krishnamurti and Martin Buber to *Aakash, FIITJEE* and *Brilliant* and they would die! Third, as a university faculty begins to see himself/herself primarily as a 'researcher' with projects, never ending publications and 'networking', teaching suffers. It tends to become secondary—at times, an obstacle, and a burden! In the age of utility, fame and visibility, it is not easy to live and excel as a teacher working in silence and performing wonders in the classroom.

This wonderful book tells us a different story. With a great deal of reflexivity, the authors have looked at the practice of the vocation, the meaning of being a teacher, and the process of continual interaction with young learners—their cognitive/intellectual trajectories, their hopes and aspirations and their hidden anxieties. Not solely that. As these sensitive teachers of Ambedkar University Delhi reflect on this meditative process, they rediscover themselves as human souls enriched by empathy and the art of listening. In a way, writing becomes therapeutic. It is great to be enchanted when a teacher writes:

> Often when I have asked myself what it means to be a teacher, an image has returned to me. I see a landscape, perhaps a garden, perhaps an open piece of land, strewn with invisible but living seeds that sprout here and there into

> tiny leaves and grass, little shrubs, moderate size plants and magnificently looming trees. This non-homogenized garden grows at its own pace, facilitated as it is by the life imparting sources of nature within whose lap it resides. The forms of energy that develop roots within this piece of earth have an intimate relationship with the seeds from which they spring forth, as also with the provisions of care and facilitating conditions of nature that make it possible for each of them to reach their potential flowering. Our classrooms too are like this piece of earth.

I find myself in the book. I find co-travellers undertaking a similar journey. I celebrate it. I celebrate when one tries to 'empathetically connect with students. I celebrate when one undertakes a 'personal journey to the inner worlds of students with their familial, socio-historical identities'. It arouses hope. It cultivates my faith in the interplay of affect and cognition'. It is good to be reminded once again that a university is about 'reason, compassion and creativity'.

I do admit that things are not easy; the obstacles are enormous. I see the all-pervading media simulation with its unholy alliance of Bollywood, cricket and corporate elites mythologizing the narratives of 'success'. I see the rise of the 'authoritarian personality'. I see the reduction of children into 'exam warriors'. I see a regimented culture of surveillance, bureaucratic control and technical 'efficiency' with its inherent hostility to the spirit of dialogue, communication, creative exploration and critical thinking. In other words, I see a form of cultural politics that suspects all that is great about life-affirming teaching—freedom, trust, pluralism and the quest for a compassionate world. Not solely that. I visualize the coming danger. As the lure of information revolution, intoxication with fancy gadgets, the seduction of virtual intimacy and instantaneity of 'online' communication tend to insulate us from the physical reality of the embodied human community, classroom as a vibrant site of learning is in crisis. Is it that the empty classroom is becoming the new normal? But then, I insist that meaningful teaching is not about information. A teacher is not a quizmaster. A vibrant classroom is a sacred space. It has its fragrance; the presence of the teacher in communion with young minds is a piece of poetry. Technology cannot replace it. A teacher ought to have faith in his/her mission and vocation. It is only a sensitive teacher who can understand the desperation in the poignant phrace: 'only connect'. And it is only a teacher who is a believer in the profound art of listening who can say: 'I have heard personal stories around making career options, diseases, family discord, rape, sexual abuse, molestation, death and loss.'

The present book gives us this hope in love and care, and in knowing and healing. A teacher, let me repeat, is not merely a scholar burdened with knowledge; she/he carries a lamp that enchants the souls of young learners. A book of this kind is a refreshing departure from the routinized academic publications. It ought to be read by all those who have not yet lost their dream of meaningful education, and is engaged with teaching and the beauty of teacher-taught relationship.

Avijit Pathak
Professor/CSSS/SSS/JNU
New Delhi

Acknowledgements

This book owes its existence to the interbeing of students and teachers. The work also heavily draws on the actual space of the classroom that holds students and teachers together and within whose vibrant culture and safe walls, discussions and sharing of knowledge and experiences take place. The Centre of Psychotherapy and Clinical Research (CPCR) which initiated the dialogue with teachers to share their pedagogical vision is thankful to the larger community of Ambedkar University Delhi for their active support and faith in psychotherapy. CPCR is especially indebted to the founding Vice Chancellor, Prof. Shyam Menon for his continuing support and faith in the Centre's activities.

My thanks go to Deepti Sachdeva for taking an active role in the organization of CPCR's 2016 Mental Health Day, *Awaaz* on the theme of *Pedagogy and Psychological First Aid* and to Shefali Singh for her continuing assistance in maintaining communication with teachers. I also take this opportunity to thank Mr. C. Sajeesh Kumar for his help during the different stages in the unfolding of this process. A special heartfelt thanks is due to Mr. M.V. Kannan who has copy edited this entire book with amazing patience and commitment. Much gratitude is also due to Mr. K.K. Saxena and Aakar Books for publishing the book with care and serious involvement.

The photo images which add to the subtle beauty of the book are a gift from Shyam B. Menon, Ananya Kushawa and Dimple (Amreen) Oberoi Vahali. I thank them for enhancing the aesthetic quality of this volume with much delicacy and depth.

The spirit of the book lies in the openness and authenticity with which the contributors have expressed their deeper strivings and dilemmas of being teachers and practising challenging modes of relating with students both within and outside of the classroom. Their writings come together to create a confluence, ever so impactful in its rhythmic orchestration. The spirit of this work resides equally in our students. As we travel together with them in the journey of life, we too grow along with them. It is to them that we owe our identity of being teachers. Without them, we could have not known or realized so many crucial aspects of our being. In writing about students, let me also mention all those young people who could have been our students, but who could not gain entry into the gates of a university due to unequal social conditions. The 'absent-presence' of these potential young lives pricks our conscience and adds to our sense of responsibility.

On a more personal note, as one amongst others who has had the good fortune of giving shape to the Centre of Psychotherapy and Clinical Research, and as someone who held the dream of this book becoming a reality someday, let me take a moment to pause and express my gratitude to several teachers, mentors and work partners who have brought enrichment to my experiences in the field of higher education. Somewhere at the back of my mind, they informed my reveries and explorations, even as I visualized this work finding its present form.

From Krishwar Shirali, my teacher in Master's at Himachal Pradesh University, I learnt that education is not limited to what is written in text books but is an endeavor to engage with issues in the real world. Her passion to understand the lives of women, to intervene in rural contexts and to enliven the subject matter of a gender-sensitive psychology as a living process has stayed with me and influenced my own explorations as a teacher. From G.G. Prabhu, who was my teacher at the National Institute of Mental Health and Neuro Sciences (NIMHANS) Bangalore, I imbibed the value of hard work and discipline, of infusing every effort with excellence and of meeting each patient with utmost sincerity. From R. Raghuram, my professor of Psychiatry at NIMHANS, I learnt to listen patiently to those in deepest despair and psychological confusion. His capacity to relate to grossly troubled mental patients and to sift out from that garbled communication, salient subjective themes of crucial relevance to their lives, was a lesson which has stayed on in my mind far beyond those early years of my youth. Uma H., my supervisor in child psychotherapy, nurtured the value of kindness, care and devotion. Her work symbolized what it meant to patiently wait for the child to grow and to continue loving the child in spite of challenges. As I look back today, I also remember Dr. Jaidev with much gratitude. Though I was never taught by him directly, his dedication and inspiring presence as a teacher have influenced me in so many subtle ways.

From Ashok Nagpal, I learnt the importance of self-reflection. During the last twenty-three years of our work together, he has exemplified teaching through a free associative process. His classes are imbued with a rare mystical quality, often birthing new and creative ideas of value to the pulsating joys and struggles of becoming human.

In Shyam Menon, I have witnessed what all it takes to create a collective ethos of envisioning higher education as a simultaneous process of intellectual enrichment and compassionate caring. Working across universities with him in the last eighteen years, I have held in deep regard his 'maternal' devotion, daring spirit and attentive dedication in facilitating a value-based culture of education. As a visionary dreamer he has instilled in many the dream that the classroom is a nursery of memories, and the university a preparatory ground for students to learn to swim far beyond mainstream currents.

From Diamond, I have imbibed the ethic of enduring humanism. Her delicate regard and sensitive reception of every student's life has been inspirational for me. Her devotion and creativity as a teacher has touched me in innumerable ways. I have learnt much from her exploration of the human condition through literature and cinema.

Dimple (Amreen) has made me ever so mindful of the fact that teaching is a relationship which can only flourish in mutuality. She has functioned as that part of my inner conscience which questions the implicit power and hierarchy in the teacher-student bond and which self-consciously strives to develop it into a blossoming mutuality.

I have reached moments of silent appreciation as well as ecstatic joy in participating in the teaching-learning context with some of my former students who are now my colleagues at the School of Human Studies (SHS) and at CPCR. With them I am relearning what it means to stay committed to students in spite of all kinds of challenges. They are also helping me to ingather, in a quieter mode, a way of listening to that which desperately seeks expression by students. Our joint celebration of education as a journey is infused with meaning and ever fresh challenges.

I thank Santosh, Minakshi and Sandeep. They have taught me that for the classroom to become a vibrant space, so much of active work and silent effort of those working in university offices has to be in place first and foremost.

A special tribute to my students. As I look back I remember so many presences who for the last two decades have enlivened my classroom and also my life. Too numerous to be named here, I thank each one of them for creating me into the teacher that I am still in the process of becoming!

I thank my parents and grandparents who were the first and most significant teachers of my life, as well my brother Preet Oberoi and my uncles, Harinder Singh Vahali and T.S. Oberoi for their continuing care and support.

This is also the moment to express my gratitude to all the people who visit us at the psychotherapy clinic. They impart to us the most precious relational gift as they entrust their inner lives to our care. They teach us to be students of those human parts which call for holding and love.

This work is thus a collective effort, owing itself to all of the above persons, moments of interaction, and structural and institutional processes within which the *beautiful being of teaching* and the teacher student-relationship breathe with life and vibrancy.

No man can reveal to you aught but that which already lies half asleep in the dawning of your knowledge....

If he is indeed wise he does not bid you enter the house of his wisdom, but rather leads you to the threshold of your own mind.

—Khalil Gibran

Introduction

In our attempts to make sense of the phenomenal and material reality, there is a rich realm of knowledge emerging from intellect and rationality which we take for granted. This is based on abstractions and meta-theorizations drawn from prolonged observations and engagement. There is also another form of knowing born from and leading to experiential knowledge that comes from the living of our life. In the first instance this may strike us as intuition, protoideas, pre-conceptions or unexplainable emotional connections. It may take long periods in the life of an individual or of a culture to sift out experientially significant formulations from this precious mine. Both the former and the latter sources of relating to the world are in fact deeply interconnected, creating a unique self-reflexive capacity in humans.

The history of higher education is however marked by a rift between these two modes of understanding. In most of its institutional forms, universities and other formal educational bodies have prioritized conceptualizations which are scientific, rational, logical, graspable, definable, knowable and conscious. In this process, the irrational and the non-rational, the humane, the unconscious, 'unknowable' and emotive aspects of engaging with the self and the other have been relegated to the margin. In consequence arts, social sciences and humanities have often been pejoratively considered as 'soft' and 'feminine' and thus of vague, inferior and insignificant value. As a result, to lesser or greater degrees, the place of the subjective, relational and interpersonal has been pushed to the periphery in these streams too. In their quest for recognition as valid knowledge forms, they also have, at times, embraced the rational and the critical by distancing themselves from emotional and experiential modes of immersed engagement.

At another level, higher education in India is today threatened by the power of the market. Along with this comes the prospect of its increasing commercialization and privatization as the State too is keen to abdicate its responsibility of funding and supporting educational institutions and universities. The field of education, like that of health, is facing a serious challenge. The public health system in India has over time become more or less redundant in offering quality care to the majority of citizens who cannot afford the high costs involved in private health care. The crisis is aggravated as the middle and upper classes have given up on the government health system and thus reduced its answerability to the people who could in fact demand accountablitiy. A similar trend seems to be underway in the field of education too. As the middle and upper classes choose to send their children to private institutions and as the government withdraws its support, education also faces the possibility of becoming an 'industry' (driven by the demands of the market) where only the wards of the elite and the rich will ultimately enter.

In addition to the above developments, coupled with the race for careerism and professionalism in our times, over—reliance on productivity, personal success and ambition have obscured the imagination of education as a communion of minds and beings, the classroom as an interdependent field of charged interpersonal moments between the teacher and students and teaching-learning as an ethical-political-relational process. Strong and rigid ideological identification of teachers has further pushed exploration and engagement to the periphery of classrooms. We have also lost much by giving up the fantasy of teaching as a process birthing a spirit of playfulness and freedom of thought through the beauty of surprise. Words such as empathy and understanding have increasingly been removed from classroom spaces, apart from disciplines such as Education, Psychology, Design, Arts and Aesthetics and Literature, amongst a few others. A shadow of suspicion and impatience is cast on efforts that consider the teacher's role in the university as a facilitator and coparticipant enabling her students' growth through delicate devotion and maternal-like nurturance. This is looked upon with disdain as being unprofessional and non-scientific.

It is needless to reiterate that most notions informing critical education consider intellect as a pursuit of the mind which is far removed from the furtherance of humane attributes such as the inculcation of sensitivity, consideration for others and self, empathy, compassion and growth via cooperation. This divide between rationalist-intellectual and humanist-relational pursuits has potentially endangered streams of higher education and even, practice in the social and medical sciences, to be gripped by 'affectless-thinking', a grasping after 'pure objectivity' and 'dry intellectualization'.

At Ambedkar University Delhi (AUD), in contradistinction to the above, we have been fortunate to have a vision of higher education in which teaching can still sometimes be rendered as a song with rhythmic flows. Here, concerns for the subjective life of the student as well as the cherishment of her intellectual and critical faculties have been considered as twin pillars to be simultaneously strengthened. This is reflected in the vision statement of the university in unequivocal terms. It is also evident in the salience which has been accorded to integrating education and classroom situations with issues related to mental health and emotional transformation. Setting up a Centre of Psychotherapy and Clinical Research (CPCR) and encouraging its vitalizing advancement bears testimony to the university's commitment to attending to the psychic life of the student and creatively reimagining the teacher-student relationship as well.

One of the wings of CPCR is the *ehsaas* psychotherapy clinic. For the past several years, those of us who are trained in psychotherapy have been attending to real life issues of students within the safe and vibrantly alive confines of the clinical space. Stories of life belonging to unmet and/or birthing desires of young individuals including but not limited to their sexual, gender identity and affective preoccupations, conflicts emerging from familial spaces, inequalities and social discriminations marking their personal histories and the transitions in subjectivity heralded by classroom discourses impregnate the living walls of the clinic with *ehsaas*– poignant emotional affects—even as they enthral the psychotherapist's keen ear with resonances which have a long-lasting impact.

With particular reference to the teaching process, these pulsating reverberations of *ehsaas* include hesitant narrations of what is neglected, what is put down and also sometimes brutally crushed in classrooms. There are also stories about the classroom serving as a creative transitional space wherein via critical pedagogy, students are encouraged to rethink their relationships with their society, culture, family and self. This process of self-questioning and introspection is often an intense and difficult one. The ripples of turbulence generated in the classroom, even as they are in service of the future growth of the student, experienced even momentarily are difficult to bear. Students walk into the psychotherapy clinic with much chaos and confusion *about who they were, who they are becoming and how best can they continue to relate to the traditional set-ups to which they culturally belong.* In many instances, the clinic becomes a reflective site of holding and containing the hermeneutics of creative self-doubt leading the young person through a revitalizing process of deep psychic exploration and personal transformation. The entire process is held in place through the compassionate holding and immersive psychological co-journeying by the therapist.

Having a psychotherapy clinic in the university does something to the vision of higher education by underlying the need for a reconsideration of the pedagogical modalities and meanings attached to the pursuit of knowledge in academic spaces. It urges the teaching-learning process to make space for receiving questions and dilemmas about lived life, the impossibilities, tragedies and joyful surprises of existence even as the classroom serves as a receptade for the humane in the teacher-student bond. It draws our attention to the fact that teaching for justice has to be grounded in principles of interpersonal justice. Classroom has to, first and foremost, become a site of practice where discourses on transformative politics have to be accompanied by a reception of the life of the student. Teachers have to 'walk their talk', that grand imaginations of politics and reverberations of radical idealism have to be tested in the authentic reception of a student's life. It is from here that theories actually begin to speak to the young learners from a heart-mind continuum and the university, continues to serve its crucial function as the register of the imaginary vistas for futures yet to unfurl.

The fact that the psychotherapy clinic is situated in a university context has decided importance for visions of therapeutic processes too. The university provides for a unique opportunity to connect themes of personal and social-political import through the personal life history of the student. In this process, the work of the psychotherapist no longer remains limited to a one-to-one understanding of psychic life. Instead in listening to any person's existence, the psychotherapist goes beyond the individualized reception of the student's life. She reaches an enhanced appreciation of the socio-political conflicts and transitions within which the emotional past of a person freely breathes or feels suffocated. Narrations about self-experience thus also symbolize that which is struggling to be articulated in classrooms, in families and/or what is held in anticipation of its birth in our society at large. Through our work as psychotherapists, we have again and again been led to appreciate the salience of classroom processes and the crucial role of teachers in facilitating growth (or obstructing the same) along the twin pillars—the intellectual and experiential dimensions in their students' lives.

This repeated invocation of the two-way mutuality between pedagogical approaches and psychotherapeutic quests encouraged us to begin speaking to teachers in AUD as early as in 2012 about their struggles and challenges, their moments of joy and anguish, their reflections on the ebbs and flows of empathetic and experiential pedagogies and the place they accorded to engaging with the entire life and context of the student. We were pleasantly surprised that several of our colleagues showed an eagerness to dwell on this theme with much interest and enthusiasm. Encouraged by their responses, in July 2016, I called upon my colleagues to write on their journeys and then in October 2016, we devotedly concentrated on the theme of *Pedagogy and Psychological First Aid* during our annual celebration *Awaaz*, an attempt to commemorate the World Mental Health Day[1]. It was heartening to note that more than fifteen teachers of AUD from several disciplinary backgrounds came forward to share their thoughts, ideas, ethics and ideals on teaching as a process inclusive of receiving the psychic world of the student. Teachers shared their dilemmas, and also moments of relational success and failures—all in an attempt to self-reflexively relook at their professional and humane roles. They also highlighted how this led to a deepening of their identities and the self-transformations this brought about in consequence.

This volume is the culmination of the work done by the Centre of Psychotherapy and Clinical Research in association with teachers of AUD to foster a sensitive teaching climate in the University. It is a coming together of our joint efforts in rethinking the empathetic and critical approaches to education. The book is divided into six sections. Each section is inclusive of writings that resonate with particular nuances and strivings through which the classroom is imbibed with vitality and

1. Pedagogy and Psychological First Aid was the global mental health theme for 2016. We decided to dedicate our annual Mental Health Day Awaaz 2016 to a furtherance of the theme. Here I wish to make a special mention of Deepti Sachdeva, Assistant Professor of Psychology, School of Human Studies and member of CPCR under whose active organizational efforts CPCR could take this challenge to its potential promise. I also wish to thank all other members of the Centre of Psychotherapy and Clinical Research for their energetic involvement and passionate participation in *Awaaz* 2016.

signification. Cutting across the sections and imparting continuity to the entire volume are several searching questions and reflections of teachers engaged in writing about their immersive experiences. In the twenty six essays that bedeck this volume, teachers self-reflexively reexamine the vision, purpose and ethics involved in their profession. Some accounts are of younger teachers who began their academic career at AUD itself. Others have had much longer innings at *becoming* a teacher. They carry to AUD their memories and experiences from past institutions where they earlier taught. A majority of the reflections that follow are by facilitators in social sciences and the arts. Complementing these are interesting writings on the place of intersubjective processes in psychotherapy, design and also medical training.

Whether young or otherwise, most teachers who speak through this effort, uphold the ideal of higher education as a channel to think through questions of social justice and equity, of balancing access to education with creating opportunities of increasing participation for those from deprived backgrounds, of using the classroom as a facilitative space, and of opening the student's mind to engage with difficult questions about the self and the world. Along with the above, the writings also detail classroom processes and the strivings of teachers to actualize their professional ethics in the times when higher education is facing crises on all possible fronts—from privatization of education to its becoming an industry of capitalism. And in our times where stress on exclusivist identities has become acutely sharp, teachers and students also face the danger of becoming members of groups with opposing and sometimes antagonistic interests. A return to the ethic of care and compassionate holding in the classroom contexts, thus all the more is inbuded with a radical and subversive import today!

It is with love that the twenty-six contributors to this volume weave in a beautiful pattern in the tapestry of higher education as they sing a song that includes the missing notations of empathy in their reflections on higher education. A melody emerges as teaching is re-envisioned as an intense and involved immersive emotional experience, charged with desire, devotion and inspiration, impelling one to the freedom of spirit, to the acknowledgement of past emotional scars even as newer versions of self are born in the classroom (and disavowed ones reclaimed) through a humane and mutual exchange between the teacher and her students. As can be imagined, such writing can never be smooth and straight. *A song called teaching*, as is imaginable, has its own high and low points, its ebbs and flows; the pitch changes and so do the stresses on the notations. All of this adds to the complex beauty of the melody. Thus, the reflections remain fraught with their own necessary turbulence in the form of doubts, questions and apprehensions that teachers express in the following pages. What if we do not know how to respond to the aftereffect and lurking ripples of that which we ourselves have encouraged through forms of evocative teaching? What if the emotions unfolded in the classroom are far too much to be contained? What if we realize that we ourselves are in need of help? What if the complex issues we have gotten in touch with in the students' lives have no possibility of resolution? The writers in this volume take us through their active struggles as teachers, openly share their vulnerabilities and fears and in the process offer methods of rejuvenation to the teaching-learning process. The hesitation and the lack of surety in the teacher's voice adds to the value of this volume.

This is the first time that teachers from different disciplinary backgrounds in AUD have come together to reflect on their preoccupations with a form of teaching where the life of the student too is considered as of consequence; her particular life stage, past experiences and contexts are valued, and also the unequal situations which mar her history are sensitively related to. The teachers contributing to this series of writings believe that this enables them to uphold the conviction that education can serve its socially corrective and radical role by not only facilitating a critical mindset propelling the student towards an ethical and just world but also by nurturing them to grow in ways which are considerate and non-competitive.

An authentic relatedness through deep listening and the acknowledgement of one's vulnerabilities by the teacher carry a far greater potential to inspire growth in the student than other methods. In effect, this work proposes a form of learning by empathizing, entering the world of the other through sympathetic imagination and the cherishment of deep reflection. This mutuality of relatedness in the teaching-learning situation depends on the capacity for creative self-doubt and introspection in both teachers and students. Pedagogy is a crucial concern here and meditation on it invokes the notations of a melodious song. Committed to a relational journey in teaching, even as teachers sing to an empathetic tune, their involvement creates conditions such that *a song called teaching* begins to flow with its rhythmic ebbs and flows.

Honey Oberoi Vahali

Section 1
Beautiful Being of Teaching

All I ever wanted was to reach out and touch another human being not just with my hands but with my heart.

— Tahereh Mafi

Photo credit: Shyam B. Menon

1

On Teaching[1]

Shyam B. Menon

> I have learned that people will forget what you said, people will forget what you did, but people will never forget how you made them feel.
>
> —Maya Angelou

The popular conception about school and university is that they are spaces where young people pick up their intellectual and social skills, their language, their knowledge capital and their friendship networks. What we often choose to ignore is that school and university are primarily the nursery of memories—memories of experiences of intense human engagement, communion with self and environment, interpersonal spaces and social spaces—good and bad memories, happy and sad memories. And we know that we all have a selective memory. As educators we need to remember that classrooms can easily become the breeding ground of cultures of fear leading to an accumulation of painful and stressful memories in students. This awareness can inspire a teacher to remain committed to creating an environment of empathy, sympathetic imagination,

1. These ideas are truly not mine alone. These have got crystallized over the years through conversations, reflections and collective actions among friends and colleagues. Hopefully, these are held and developed collectively among many of us as *interbeings*. I am particularly indebted to my friend and colleague Professor Honey Oberoi Vahali for helping me find expression for some of the ideas contained in this piece.

mutual respect and even care and love in the classroom context. This could become an integral aspect of the professional ethics of teachers.

To a considerable extent, it is the memories of how school and university made one feel, or for that matter, how one's family and peers made one feel, that eventually determines the extent to which one accepts certain aspects of oneself or ends up living in constant shame and denial of those aspects. There is enough evidence to support the view that seeking of violent solutions to crises in life can be causally traced to how we were made to feel during our infancy, childhood and youth. The seeds for taking to violent ways later in life, whether it is physical violence or emotional violence, whether it is violence in a larger social or political context or violence within the family, are often sown in the manner in which our vulnerable childhoods and youths are held, respected, ridiculed or exposed. When we expose and humiliate little children and young adults in schools and universities we could make them crippled for life and also socialize them into the belief that the only way to respond to violence is through counter-violence or alternatively they live a life of low self-esteem, despondency and self-pity. Humiliation at educational institutions may not have to be overt and explicit. Indeed, it is often subtle, but injurious all the same.

In its ideal form, university is more about addressing issues related to social transformation and needs of learners and less about responding to market demands. Its core processes and messages are about reason, compassion and creativity. When new ideas need to be germinated, they need a nursery, a trial ground. That is what university provides. It offers a protected space for interrogating commonsense, pushing the envelope of popular sensibilities little by little, breaking new frontiers, slowly and tentatively, in the ways of thinking and feeling. It nurtures divergences. More than anything else, university provides a space for humanism and compassion. It trains young people to give voice to the voiceless. But it also encourages them to interrogate their own selves and to question the very structures they are born and socialized into. All the above put together is 'higher learning' that a university is mandated for. However, 'higher learning' sometimes also leaves young people in intense personal struggles to deal with altered (and sometimes, fractured) realities about their selves and their contexts that they have coconstructed in university. Perhaps, this is the inevitable lifelong struggle that goes always with growing up and continuing to live as thinking, reflective, creative and compassionate people.

It takes an enormous lot to create a collective ethos of envisioning higher education as a simultaneous process of intellectual enrichment and compassionate caring. This requires that we keep alive the faith and daring to think beyond the social givens and to respond to every challenging situation in an innovative manner. The envelope of intellectual change has to be pushed gradually. Else, it can create major disjunctions in the mind space of young people. Along with a vision of education, as a transformative process, we will also need to keep in mind that the emotional life and context of every student counts. Even as universities are preparatory spaces for responding to social needs they are also nurturing grounds of enabling students, who in the future will identify and find ways to respond to vacuums of human needs in collective social life.

I started my teaching career in the early 1980s in a large unitary university located in a district town in Western India. When I first entered the classroom as a teacher, I was myself a young research scholar. I prepared well for my classes, and I thought I was quite effective in my articulation. I was in a self-congratulatory mode. One day, a set of students in my class came up to me and said in Gujarati, "Sir, you speak so well, so eloquently that we do not understand a word of what you say!" The moment hit me. It made me realize that in my pursuit of being a good teacher, I had lost contact with my students, particularly, those occupying the margins of my class. My lectures were meant for only the brightest students, while the ones who were struggling with education had been lost to me. This critical lesson in my early years made me conscious that my own narcissism could convert me into a performer. To become a teacher I most needed to be in touch with those bored, disengaged or lost students who occupied the back benches in my class and who left their silent yet powerful imprint in the classroom—the oily patches on the back wall! These young people did not need my complex ideas, or my verbose articulation. They were longing to be reached out and understood. They needed me to come proximal to their struggles and living concerns. They were not impressed by the scholarly literature I was so eager to introduce them to. On the other hand, they were intimidated by it and were made to feel inadequate. This and similar incidents later in my professional career made me realize that teaching was about engagement and immersion. It was about engagement with and immersion into students' real life questions by the teacher and the group of learners together, and at the same time it was about utilizing the finite time available prudently to accomplish curricular objectives. This is a tall order, not easy at all to work towards. This continues to this day to be my major struggle as a teacher, and I think I have a long way more to go.

Some of my most cherished moments of being a teacher across the last nearly four decades are about spending time with my students, fostering their growth in diverse ways, talking about life and participating in the ongoing issues plaguing them. I do not hesitate in confronting them or playfully urging them to push the limits of their comfort zone a little further, of questioning the social givens, of experimenting with ideas and of enhancing their capacity for sympathetic imagination. The classroom is a space where difference and dissent can be voiced and also contained. I am sometimes quick to react, and I kick myself for not having gotten rid of this impulsive behaviour after all these years. But, I am equally eager to seek forgiveness quickly from my students. This often makes me appear to my students as somewhat vulnerable but also approachable. Over the years, I have realized that being seen as vulnerable is a small price for retaining one's spontaneity, being oneself and trying always to maintain authenticity in my relations with my students. My students have always been kind and understanding, even when they disapproved of some of my decisions, including my taking up administrative assignments. I have been very fortunate in this respect.

A lot of what I am as a teacher has come to me from my own teachers, both at school and at college. I was lucky that I grew up in another world, the world of small towns in India of the sixties and the seventies of the last century where practically all resources were in scarce supply, except (thankfully) time! And that made all the difference. The most happening place in town was my school and my college (both government-run institutions) and the most interesting people I had ever met were some of my teachers. And these teachers (and there were quite a few of them) had all the time and the eagerness to be with us discussing books, movies, politics and our lives. One learnt invaluable lessons through these interactions, lessons in care and compassion as well as in reason, finer sensibilities, listening patiently to other points of view, to defer judgements, to argue without being acrimonious and to disagree without having to be disagreeable.

Thankfully, the ethos of 'publish or perish' had not reached its ascendancy when I began my teaching career. Therefore, teaching and research seldom appeared to me (and to my peers too, I believe) as mutually exclusive and competing dimensions of work. Much of what I did by way of research found reflection in what I taught, perhaps also because I had the advantage of working in a university where teachers themselves developed course structures and did student assessment too. Often, classroom discussions led to interesting research ideas.

I have had the good fortune of teaching mostly in teacher education institutions where teaching and learning are themselves central themes of inquiry and scholarly exploration. I have had the opportunity to experience and explore various aspects of teaching and learning in the entire continuum of education, viz., primary schooling to doctoral research. This exposure has enabled me to see learning as a process of seamless continuity across life stages and has emboldened me to imagine new kinds of institutional cultures, curricular structures and processes, and new configurations of conditions supporting learning. Through this hands-on experience, I became increasingly convinced that rationality and relationality as well as compassion and creativity could go together in building an institutional culture conducive for learning of a high order. All this came very handy later while leading a team designing a new university when I was assigned such a task. I used to offer a couple of courses in the part-time Master's programme meant largely for practising school teachers. Those highly motivated school teachers, who after long days at school had to spend their precious evening hours with us at the university driven by their sheer determination to stay afloat professionally, were always a source of great inspiration and learning for me.

The years I spent on the faculty of the largest open university in India was a major hiatus in my teaching. Without a direct engagement with students, I felt a bit like a fish out of water, a feeling that eventually prompted me to return to a university where direct human engagement with students was possible. Having said that, those years also enabled some very useful learning. Open university system entailed a large team working in close coordination comprising academics, instructional designers, media professionals and a whole range of people engaged in such complex operations such as publishing, producing television programmes, managing online systems, distributing course material, student support, etc. The focus of this complex operation was the student at a distance attempting on her own to learn. I learnt once again that the learner and not the teacher was the major protagonist in education. I learnt that teaching in an organized system was not just about individual virtuosity of the teacher, but that a whole array of others had to work behind scenes, unseen and unacknowledged, for a good teacher to do her work effectively.

In the later years, I was interacting more and more with MPhil and PhD scholars through a course in qualitative research methods that I used to offer. While the 'methodology' courses often tended to become somewhat dry and drab and a little detached from ground realities, we (my students and I) had over the years fashioned our course to include its own practicum where the students had to do a small piece of research based on a brief fieldwork. The credo of the course was on research as a means to amplify the voice of the voiceless. Colearning this course along with the MPhil and PhD scholars has been a great learning experience for me. Our classes often took a study circle mode reading a text together, and I have learnt a great deal in this process from my students.

For the past about ten years now, all my time has been getting consumed by tasks related to working in teams setting-up, governing and administering a university. I have not had a chance of engaging in classroom teaching for a long time now. While I miss direct involvement in the core activity of enabling learning, I have also begun to understand the importance of establishing and sustaining institutions, structures, processes and conventions that enable the nurturance of a healthy institutional culture without which it is difficult for the core activities of teaching and learning to happen. It is imperative that the nature of university as a self-governing community of scholars needs to be preserved. This means, administrative and organizational matters need participation and oversight by the faculty. Towards the realization of this, a teacher will also need to devote part of her time to matters of governance and administration. The challenge, of course, is for her not to lose touch in this process with the ground realities of students' lives.

Although I have not been 'practising' as a classroom teacher this past decade, I have had a very special ringside view of the world of teachers and students because of the office I have been holding. I have had long and intense conversations on matters related to teacher-student relationships with students as well as teachers. I realize that the teaching-learning contexts have transformed drastically in myriad ways since the turn of the millennium. Because of the regimen related to professional progression, such as the stipulations by the University Grants Commission, teachers are becoming increasingly conscious of the ways in which their time gets apportioned between teaching and research. Research and publishing are encouraged by the system, often at the cost of humane teacher-student engagement. The new system encourages teachers to perceive themselves primarily as producers of knowledge and only peripherally (if at all) as mentors nurturing the potential of compassionate growth, critical intellect and sensibilities in students. I have also painfully witnessed situations in bodies like Academic Council where teachers have closed ranks on issues where students have alleged lack of fairness and justice. In such occasions, sadly, teachers tend to depict students in adversarial terms.

On the part of students too, there have been some disquieting trends. Firstly, in an age of identities based on exclusion (in our contemporary times, along the lines of caste and gender), students sometimes get into the mode of self-righteous assertion that challenges the relational dynamics of teachers and students. Students often resent teachers' care and concern, perceiving it to be patronizing. Secondly, young people in our times are increasingly living a dual life shuttling between real and virtual worlds of social and human engagements. The ubiquitous influence of social media in the lives of young people has made a deep impact on the core processes of teaching and learning and the teacher-student relationship. Thirdly, higher education in the post-liberalization political economy is seen critically connected with job placements and mobility in economic status. In this context, there is an increasing tendency to characterize teacher-student relationship as a professional-client engagement in an instrumentalist sense.

In spite of all this, the teacher often turns out to be an immensely influential, sometimes inspiring, presence in the lives of many students, particularly in certain critical stages of their development. Teachers touch their lives in crucial ways in their most formative years. This role of the teacher—often assumed willingly, but sometimes just ascribed and taken on reluctantly—comes invariably with considerable power. I think, the teacher should be acutely conscious of the power she wields, and must be careful to exercise it with utmost responsibility. The challenge is to keep the nurturing role alive while being mindful that one's involvement does not become emotionally overwhelming for the student. Notwithstanding the human dimension of teacher-student relationship, which is characterized as much by compassion and sensitivity as by rationality and intellectual curiosity, I am convinced that, there have to be boundaries that should define the extent of its intensity. After all, the teacher-student relationship is mediated by complex institutional structures, legal obligations, rights and so on. Boundaries set by codes of ethics for teachers and codes of conduct for students are as much essential elements that characterize teaching and learning as compassion and intellectual rigour are.

Learning is an integral element in the basic functions of humans. For as long as human civilization has existed, there have been institutional manifestations mandated to facilitate learning among younger members of society. Such facilitation may have been through engagement and interaction among peer learners or between learners and the 'learned'. In every society and in every historical period, there have been social contrivances constituted of institutional contexts and programmatic structures within which learning is facilitated, supervised, supported and accorded recognition. So long as learning in organized settings remains an essential feature of growth, development, socialization and enculturation of young humans, teaching as a second order category of facilitating learning will continue to be one of the core activities central to human civilization. Specific dynamics of teaching may vary from epoch to epoch, or from one historical period to another, but its essential character will remain intact. To my mind, the strains and stresses that we experience today in the profession and the vocation of teaching are nothing unprecedented—every period in history must have seen such turbulences. While adapting to the requirements of the shifting contexts of learning and its changing nature, we must ensure that teaching does not lose touch with its own core values of humanism and compassion.

2

The Beautiful Being of Teaching

Diamond Oberoi Vahali

One of the most important functions of a teacher, in my perspective, is to hold students and to nurture them. Unfortunately, most teachers and students feel that teaching is a detached exercise and talking to students, engaging and relating to their lives is a waste of time and is not an intrinsic part of education. Increasingly, the entire thrust of education is towards the development of intellect and on understanding the mind of students in relation to a text or a given theoretical framework. Sadly, education does not work in the direction of cherishing growth, by connecting theoretical frameworks and texts to the experiences of students. In my experience of being a teacher for the past twenty-five years, I have come to the realization that teaching that connects to the lives of students goes deep into their psyche and being. Apparently, like several teachers, some students too may feel that this kind of teaching is not as relevant as the one in which a lot of information and theoretical perspectives are introduced and developed. In retrospect, some of them may reach the realization that classes which had left an indelible mark on their experiential being were actually the ones which were the most transformative. Education based on information and facts, may help students to pass examinations and prepare them for jobs (of course this too is very important) but it falls short of transforming the being of a person. According to me, the meaning of education and its purpose is to open up the minds of people to newer perspectives and to challenge old ways of thinking, or rigid consolidated ways of being. Education thus has to touch and transform a person from deep within.

If as teachers, we open our classes to a different kind of pedagogy which is inclusive of emotions, the entire texture of teaching and classroom interaction undergo a change. Teaching by connecting with the experiences of students is one of the best means of communication. I would like to share my experience of teaching two courses at the Master's level and one course at the BA level, in Ambedkar University Delhi. The titles of the MA English courses are, 'Analysing Fiction: The Human Condition', and 'European Cinema and the Exploration of the Human Psyche'. The BA English course is titled, 'Modern Short Fiction and Novellas'. 'Analysing Fiction: The Human Condition' has been offered twice so far by me. The first time I had offered it was in the Winter semester 2013 and the second time, in the Monsoon semester 2014. European cinema course was offered for the first and the only time in the Monsoon semester 2015. 'Modern Short Fiction and Novellas' has been offered twice so far. Though I have taught a number of other courses in AUD, yet it is these three courses which have left the most lasting impression on the minds of my students.

'Analysing Fiction: The Human Condition', is a course that deals with very few texts. It centres around three novels: Toni Morrison's *The Bluest Eye,* Thomas Hardy's *The Mayor of Casterbridge* and Albert Camus's *The Fall* and five short stories and novellas, Mohan Rakesh's '*Miss Pal*', Fyodor Dostoevsky's '*The Meek One*', Franz Kafka's '*Metamorphosis*', Flaubert's '*The Legend of St Julian the Hospitaller (Three Tales)*' and Qadiryar's '*Qissa Puran Bhagat*'. We also include a number of other related texts through student presentations, but the main thrust of the course is on these eight narratives. There is nothing very unique about these texts, but the pedagogy of the course is different than what is normally followed. The themes that the course takes up are those concerning the concept of beauty and ugliness, racism and self-loathing, love and hatred, the dynamics of power in relationships, disability and the paradigm of productivity, power and the quest to transcend it, life and death, neglect and the guilt that comes with it and a deeper quest for forgiveness and spirituality. Each text is dealt with a lot of nuance and detail. Since the course is about the human condition, we follow the life history of the protagonists from the beginning of their lives and try to see and understand why they behave and act in a certain manner and how they became the persons that they did. We try to follow their life journey and see the reasons behind their deeds. In the process, we experience the pain and suffering of these characters. The interaction in the classes is largely experiential as I ask the course participants to connect with the characters through their subjective experiences. I begin each new narrative by asking them to tell me what they felt when they read the story. What was their response to the characters, what did the characters evoke in them? Did they feel anger, love, irritation, hatred, pity, sympathy or empathy for the characters? I ask them to look within and tell me why they felt what they felt, and see how their feelings change as they begin to engage with the narrative more deeply. Gradually, as we do a second reading of the same narrative, we look at the changing shades of our emotions and so on and so forth. The entire course is centred on discussions. As a collective we try to figure out and make meaning about the lives of the characters. In the process of analysing the stories, students deeply resonate with the narratives and many a time begin to share their lives, sometimes directly and sometimes indirectly. Eventually, the atmosphere of the entire classroom is transformed into a mode akin to that of a group therapy experience wherein there is an invisible centre, that of a teacher as a facilitator and around this centre are numerous students sharing their experiences. It is through their sharing that unwittingly they offer therapeutic help without even being aware of how they are assisting each other's life by opening up their own lives.

The most important aspect that takes birth in the process is of listening to each other. It is through listening, that healing takes place. A few students, in certain moments also experience minor breakdowns as the themes of the stories speak closely to their lives. Sometimes in the beginning of the course, a few experience the course to be too heavy and find it difficult to cope with it. But gradually, as the course develops and gains momentum, as we travel from one narrative to another, students begin to realize that the stories they are dealing with are not so much about the life of someone out there but are also about their lives. Different students relate to different stories and to different aspects of the course.

For assessment, I request them to maintain a journal in which I ask them to make an entry everyday after the class. I do not expect them to write volumes but I expect that they will get back and reflect on the class discussions especially the parts that they could connect to. I ask them to free associate in their journals and later if they feel that something too personal has been shared, they can just seal the page which I will not open. Some students write extensively, they write short notes on each story and a lot about their emotions, others write very little. I do not evaluate them on the length of their journals but on the adequate ways in which they have been able to receive the narratives and themes that are floated in the class.

Since this course is called 'Analysing Fiction', we also delve deep into theoretical issues. In the process, we touch upon ways of analysing texts and reading symbols; that is reading beyond the apparent into the depths of the soul. We analyse dialogues; the language of a narrative and see meanings beyond the stated. We try to understand, that since all speech is an attempt at communication, humans find it really hard to communicate and to understand and to be understood; that what actually gets communicated is only the tip of an iceberg and that a lot is left unstated. It is the unstated, the unsaid and therefore the unheard which is to be heard and arrived at, if we want to truly listen to and understand others. The thrust of the course is to reach beyond the apparent and to cultivate a non-judgemental model of listening to the lives of others. As our own being begins to resonate in different ways with others, we begin to listen to the unstated lives of characters, who are actually people, whom we have known all along in our lives but somehow have hardened towards, as we have hardened towards our own selves. We learn to become more patient about understanding the lives of people around us.

The trajectory of the 'European Cinema' course is similar; the only difference is that when I offered the 'Analysing Fiction' course for the second time, I felt that one or two students had minor breakdowns as some of the readings resonated deeply with the more painful aspects of their lives. As the course facilitator, I suffered extreme predicament and wondered if I should have offered this course at all. So the next course that I offered was similar and yet it was less intense. I focused on films this time, a medium I am passionate about. We worked on Robert Wiene's *The Cabinet of Dr. Caligari,* Luis Bunuel's and Salvador Dali's *Un Chien Andalou,* Ingmar Bergman's *Wild Strawberries,* Alain Resnais's *Hiroshima Mon Amour,* Federico Fellini's *Eight And A Half,* Rainer Werner Fassbinder's *In a Year with Thirteen Moons* and Passolini's *Oedipus Rex.* Along with each film, I did a number of theoretical readings, both related to the art of reading cinema and to films I was dealing with, specifically psychoanalytical readings. Besides, we discussed several other films through student presentations. This time I was a little more cautious.

Teaching is like walking on a razor's edge; we have to fine-tune everything lest we become lopsided. The overall results of the course were satisfactory though not overwhelming. The purpose of this course, like the previous course, was to connect to the lives of the protagonists and thus to ourselves which we were successfully able to do. We worked on themes related to memory and forgetting, love and rejection, friendship and betrayal, trauma of separation, desire and sexuality, gender and its constructs, power and resistance, love and estrangement, old age, the need to accept ourselves with the passing of time and the need for self-love and forgiveness. The assessment pattern was similar to that of the preceding course, though students were requested to add their reflections on the theoretical readings as well in the journal entries this time.

The third course 'Modern Short Fiction and Novellas' is in some ways similar to 'Analysing Fiction: The Human Condition', but in terms of the choice of themes, it is different and therefore the texture of the course is also different. I will delineate here my first experience of offering this course in 2012. The course was largely based on discussions. I asked students to subjectively respond to the stories. The narratives were not so heavy and there were no breakdowns as such. The classroom interaction was like a group therapy space once again. This group therapy was more around issues related to gender as most of these young women students brought in concerns about gender discrimination in their lives. Male students too participated intensely while responding to and understanding the restrictions and the discriminations women face. In this course somehow, perhaps as the students were younger, the overall atmosphere was lighter. We engaged a lot with each others' lives. Students connected intensely with the course and the issues that were raised. I experienced an overwhelming response and felt that even at such a formative stage, they were able to appreciate the value and the substance of literature.

In my understanding, the bonds that students develop with each other, during the process of participating in such-like courses are very strong and deep. They hone in on their ability to listen to each other and even to their own selves; they become less judgemental towards others and overall develop more understanding towards life. Some of them have come and shared with me that their perception of life has undergone a change as now they think less in terms of binaries. They have become mindful of splitting the world into good and bad and in the process are able to see the complexity under the seemingly apparent. A few of them, shared that they are trying, not to find easy solutions and have become more engaging with and tolerant of suffering: they are attempting to see a flow in things and are more open to doubt their own judgements by trying to listen to others. On the whole they have found the courses to be evocative and humanizing. The courses have also helped a few of them to become more accepting of their own selves, which I think is a crucial achievement in itself!

Every time, I have also observed that, when I offer these courses, a whole lot of students begin to open their selves up to me. My room gets flooded with students: they want to come and share their lives and problems with me. I feel overwhelmed with the kind of trust, they bring to me. They share their problems, seeking counsel. I try to tell them gently that I am not a therapist. I am aware that they understand that I am not a therapist. The reason according to me why they frequently come is because they feel held and nurtured just by being heard. I feel, half the problems of people around can be engaged with and contained by listening to them, but listening with one's entire being. Such listening is not only therapeutic, but also nurturing as well, as it holds us. And it is very important for all of us to be held in life. The more we are held, the less aggressive and judgemental we turn out to be as human beings.

When students come and share their being with me, I feel they offer the most precious gift of their lives: it is the gift of faith that I will understand them in a non-judgemental manner. In the process of talking to them, I am always afraid that I should not violate their trust in me in any way. Once or twice, I have had the experience of students just barging into my room and in under five minutes sharing and revealing the greatest secret of their lives and leaving without waiting for my response. In such moments I have felt bewildered. I have not understood how to respond. Sometimes I responded in a manner which was inappropriate, later I felt guilty and tried to rectify myself. But what is to be noted is the urgent need in people to share. I have seen that once the process opens up, then there is really no end to it; once it begins, the need to share is so intense that there is no going back on it at all.

Over the years, I have come to realize that one of the central functions of a good teacher is to listen gently in an attuned, non-judgemental manner. As teachers, we have so much been trained in speaking and delivering lectures that we tend to get divorced from a very significant aspect of teaching that is listening. How can I become a good teacher without listening to my students? How can I respond to their questions if I have not heard them in the first place? I need to listen to them with my full being, their questions; their concerns should resonate in my being if I want my teaching to touch their lives. Without properly hearing them, the music of teaching will never develop into a rhythm, and become stereophonic; teaching has to be stereophonic.

Teaching that goes into the being of students is a mode of teaching that passes through and connects with their lives. It is like the music of a flute that touches the breeze and then passes through the flute and then becomes a symphony. Teaching is also a type of music that floats through the reed of the being of a teacher; it only becomes a symphony when it touches the inner being of students and flows out. Such music, such teaching, after it has passed through the being of students, becomes unforgettable. Students may forget the details of the narratives, but what they will never forget is the essence of the narratives. As long as the essence of a story, transformed through their subjectivity, has gone deep inside them, the purpose of teaching which is touching the lives of students is complete.

Every text first has to be processed subjectively; it has to become a subjective experience before it becomes anything else. Such an encounter with a text leaves an indelible impression. I am fortunate that my discipline gives me the space to connect to the lives of people. I wish more and more disciplines were like literature and cinema, disciplines which are great encounters and dialogues with life.

In my perception, another important function of a teacher is to get involved in the lives of students by perceiving the way students talk and behave in a class. Our classes are multi-layered. They represent students from diverse linguistic, class, caste and gender groups. To assume and teach in a manner that our classes are homogeneous is a fallacy of sorts. Even while designing our courses, the diversity of the group we are teaching can become our guiding light. We can constantly modify and engage with our curriculum even during the process of transecting our courses. There is nothing that is cast in stone. There are students who come from privileged backgrounds, as there are those who come from economically, socially and emotionally impoverished backgrounds. One of my students shared with me that he lives in a slum. When I asked him if he has friends in the university, he said that though by and large people are polite with him, he really does not have any friends, and nobody really talks to him. He went on to say they could not really be his friends, as they lived in a world apart and it was very difficult for them to understand his life and the context that he came from. There are many students like him in our campus. Being part of the Students' Welfare Fund, I have been in touch with several students who feel alienated and find it difficult to connect with their economically privileged peers. Similarly there are many women students who find a total disconnect with their lives marked by acute gender discrimination and the discourses of emancipation discussed in classrooms. These discourses are emancipatory and will lead to their liberation, but constantly, we need to include their background, life histories and their lived realities into the texts that we choose to incorporate in our courses and the manner in which we transect these courses. The incorporation of the subjective and the experiential contextual domain will not only enrich our classes, but also help us to move towards a more inclusive paradigm, where teaching and our courses will become part of the lived lives and shared experiences.

3

Communicating and Not Communicating

Classroom as a Facilitating Environment[1]

Shifa Haq

On thinking about the growing capacities of babies as learners, Donald W. Winnicott, a psychoanalyst, considers maturational processes to be just as important as a facilitative environment. As a student training to be a psychotherapist one day, I became impressed with his idea of a two-person field and the necessity of play in relating to one another. One aspect of this play is a complex relation between communicating and non-communicating. To belong, to relate, is not without a deep appreciation of individuals as isolates. There exists, in each one of us, a wish to be known as well as the wish to be hidden. Nowhere else is this paradox most enigmatic than in classroom situations where a student may appear, in full continence of alertness and curiosity, while hiding a world of experiences that must go untouched in the service of intellectual growth. I see the comfort of relegating private self to silence as a primary need of an individual, immersed in a quiet exploration of inner realm, as well as a splitting between thought and feeling to make dispassionate learning possible. To me, the paradox of communicating and not communicating remains an emotionally alive field in teacher-student relationship (Winnicott, 1963). It is a potential space

1. The title of this essay owes itself to the thoughts of D.W. Winnicott, the world renowned British Psychoanalyst.

for complex subjective experiences of relatedness, or obscure arrivals, about the self and the world that carry within them the possibility of creative living.

In a course concerned with rural development and poverty, the group learns to engage with knowledge creation as it emanates from lived experiences of those engaged in it. By using a psychoanalytic frame, the group tries to look at the usefulness of staying close to subjective experiences, forms of 'knowing', that do not lend themselves easily to articulation or speech. The method of listening and attending to the feelings of co-participants in the group creates the safety required for each student to *relate* as an *isolate* ready to share what is at once personal as well as meaningful. I would like to illustrate it with an example from a classroom interaction between participants. While reflecting on the complex relation or chasm between local knowledge or personal worldviews and education, a student recounted his memory of a summer camp, where a student of fifth grade broke into tears and panic on learning about the Big Bang Theory. He added that the student felt shattered that her conception of the universe, with God's will at its genesis, was mocked and invalidated. She felt powerless and deeply alienated by this new knowledge. The class tried to make sense of the 'student from the summer camp' as an uncanny presence amidst us. A student present in this discussion began laughing uncontrollably and explained how she found the emotional outburst of the student from the summer camp extremely bizarre and funny even.

On asking her again to associate to her difficulty in connecting to the experience of the girl from summer camp, the student insisted that she could not see how a theory could be so 'earth shattering'. As a facilitator, trained in psychoanalytic practice, I was led to pursue the student's laughter as more than a dismissal of her feelings. As a group, we invited her to consider if she knew of an experience that had an 'earth shattering' meaning for her, something that her odd laughter wished to communicate. The student then began associating, in many checkered manoeuvres, the memory of her first menstruation that had an irreversible effect on her relation with her father and her brother. She felt terror at the sight of blood. The knowledge that it is normal, the expected response of the body, did not comfort her in the least. She cried for a long time, wishing that it be taken away so that she could feel like herself again. The student touched a painful part in her self and recalled the customs of segregation and isolation from her father, his body and the severing of play between them. The class became an affective repository of two young persons' profound experiences, both communicating an emotional livewire as it connected to the journey of the self, sequestered behind routine academic encounters. Following a free associative dynamic exchange between the participants in the class, the group experienced a transitional space that allowed listening anew to the seemingly unrelated, defensive styles of listening to make room for what was waiting to be articulated.

The vignette shared here is but an example of how students create and find room to bring their emotional experiences leading to an engagement with the their personal matters. This has a bearing on what we think of classrooms as spaces of knowledge building. The classroom experience for me carries the potential to open a conversation about an individual student's manner of exploring a question or inquiry, always open to an emotional storm, even if contained by the disciplined body or by disciplinary boundaries. The interplay between what one communicates and what one wishes to not communicate is also a question of inclusiveness of deeply-felt experiences that get stirred in classroom situations. A question arises: how do we engage with students' lived experiences, their location or positions, as they enter classrooms? Can theories be built on lived experiences rather than seeing them as separate? How do we listen to ourselves while we listen to others? Would this have a bearing on what a teacher wishes to undertake in a classroom and the objectives a student may have?

While there remains a big area of what is consciously avoided, work with students also reveals the challenges of much needed confrontations with what can easily be disavowed from the classroom. Much more than intellectual understanding, a student may be able to cover the distance between theory and experience when we imagine the classroom as a place to reflect on histories of trauma, marginalization and oppression. As a Muslim psychotherapist and academic, I find classroom interactions and the field of psychotherapy as a place of everyday encounter with otherness. These spaces bring home the problems of inter-subjective recognition. As I encounter the disproportionate number of students from upper class and caste backgrounds in higher education, I consciously work towards shaking the homogeneity of students to open up discussions on differences, divides and the cultures of violence to challenge normative assumptions.

In these moments, listening to the 'inappropriate' feelings or projections in the presence of the group gives the students and me a place to listen and dialogue with the affect that runs deeper than one may consiously appreciate. This is never a one-way street, with students carrying the irrational or un-nuanced ideas, but rather a dialogue in which I learn about my assumptions and *ways of seeing*. Consider for instance, a student who approached me after a class discussion on Caritas or kindness as an object of inquiry to consider who is thought of a worthy and is not worthy of kindness, and is barbaric or othered. Some students had voiced that kindness, even though potentially subversive, can be used to maintain affiliation across caste, class or religious lines. Later, after class, in our conversation with the young woman I learned through her self-disclosure, that even though she carried a Hindu name, she had converted to Islam and had a robust critique of caste system. While we continued to nod in agreement on many issues concerning the use of kindness in human relations, I was most struck by what she was helping me see. She was helping me to confront my assumptions about the classroom that I had felt so intimately acquainted with.

To relate with students, their lives, outside the university or the safety of a classroom, is to invite a conversation about challenges that often fall beyond the scope of classroom interactions. The absent student, the one 'spaced out' during a lecture or the bright stellar student, continues to participate or elude the university system while retaining an emotionally complex inner world. As a student, I often wondered whether a teacher could tell that I was not doing well. It was not until my studies in psychoanalysis that I began to see the meaning of my fantasy. I wished to be seen as 'unwell' so that my performance, the veneer of false self, could be surrendered for a more authentic contact between a teacher and me (Winnicott, 1960). Fortunately, it was not just a fantasy. Some teachers could provide background support to think and write from a place most alive, even if most difficult, in me. By taking intellectual questions closer to the internal states, issues of identity, sexuality, motivation and struggles, I was able to make sense of who I am and what are my questions. As a student I felt freer when my academic life invited experiences, challenges and struggles of young adulthood, how I viewed relationships, politics and my place in the world. It became my credo in my journey as a psychotherapist and a teacher in the university.

As a teacher and a therapist, I think of the classroom a place or a phenomenon, what Winnicott, called boundless support—there to be used as the student wishes. To learn through experiences, when unchallenged by purely intellectual questioning can create a backbone for epistemophillic instinct. In the university space, there appears to be a sharp divide over whether engagement with life of students, outside the domain of curriculum, is a vital aspect of teacher-student relationship. My experience, as a therapist, tells me that in reality, students embody the states and present them in the classroom all the time. A person undergoing a crisis, may or may not articulate her pain or distress and may even hesitate to speak about it. Like the emperor's clothes, one can mystify suffering by viewing it as a personal choice or by avoiding an authentic confrontation (Bollas, 2013). Such a stance runs the risk of making pain more alienating. It is no surprise that the more disturbed a student is, the more he or she avoids accessing structures such as the university clinic or meeting the designated authority on matters even though that may be the most effective or much needed. The episodes of breakdowns go unnoticed and as teachers, we find a sketchy description of students' underperformance. It is, therefore, imperative to think of how to appreciate the subjective experiences of persons even when they do not become the best witnesses of their own struggles. At Ambedkar University Delhi, we imagined structures such as psychotherapy clinic, equal opportunity cell, and the Students' Welfare Fund as indespensible to the vision of education. Still, it is quite possible that we fail to catch a student before he/she falls. Can the relation between a teacher and a student be a site for intervention? I feel it is happening, almost always whether or not we know of it consciously. Sometimes, it means catching a life before it disappears, sometimes a thought so that it may live.

References

1. Bollas, C. (2013). *Catch Them Before They Fall*. New York: Routledge.
2. Winnicott, D.W. (1963). Communicating and not communicating leading to a study of certain opposites. In *Maturational Processes and the Facilitating Environment: Studies in the Theory of Emotional Development*. London: Hogarth Press. pp. 179-192.
3. Winnicott, D.W. (1960). Ego distortions in terms of true and false self. In *Maturational Processes and the Facilitating Environment: Studies in the Theory of Emotional Development*. London: Hogarth Press. pp. 140-152.

4

Listening as Pedagogy and Experience as Text and Context

Ruminations of a Teacher

Vinod R.

As I sit to write this piece, I get a feeling of hesitation and fear. I realize that the fear of writing around one's pedagogical approach comes from various sources in the present as well as from past experiential struggles and residuals in becoming a teacher. Many questions loom large as I begin to ponder over them. Would this sharing reduce my teaching method and my 'teaching-being' to a technique? Will this recounting of experiences induce in me vulnerability vis-à-vis my past and the journeys travelled so far? Will I feel redundant as a teacher in the future? Will my classroom space, one of the few spaces of my agency, be hereafter governed by gaze of surveillance, power and authority? Mine is an inter-disciplinary journey of a nomad who traverses the ground between the disciplines of education and psychology. I create my own pedagogy of listening and receiving, in particular, of receiving the sense of life from the margins which in turn dwells in its own alienation and struggle for survival. My striving is to listen to voices from the margins despite the collapse of the romantic ideals of equality and justice in the existing socio-political scenario.

Pedagogic experiences in their very nature are teaching-learning processes in action. They are about receiving flows of experience, intensity, pain, authenticity and surviving ordinariness in all its complexities. I often ask myself the question: can a compilation of good and bad practices of pedagogies with all their attendant issues freeze the creativity and problem solving of teachers to work through everyday moments of practice? In other words, it is not an easy task for a teacher to write on pedagogy. Any attempt at an authentic sharing of the teaching-learning process also exposes the limits of one's being and practice and the structures of the university at which one practises one's pedagogy. The authenticity in communication in pedagogy comes with reflexivity around one's ideals and their limits. I have realized that an opening in the emotional spectre of learning for the teacher comes through when the teacher and students survive the transference and counter transference in their engagement with experience. In this process, there are silences that one learns to bear, and there are excesses of emotions that one speaks about as some experiences produce intense resonances and evoke the quality as well as limits of one's being human.

I have often felt that the 'rescue fantasy' (a desire to be there for one's students in such a manner that teaching could heal their past wounds) in a teacher seems to have a developmental trajectory. Gripped by this fantasy, a teacher metaphorically moves through various life stages of engagement such as infancy, adolescence, adulthood and old age. When I mention infancy here, it is the active agency of the teacher to take on the issues of students with complete zeal and enthusiasm in one's belief of transforming them. In this stage, there may be little fear or awareness of a sense of burnout. During the adolescent phase, the teacher continues to relate to the students in spite of all risks involved. Adult-like commitment is characterized by some restraint and in the old age phase a teacher is left with essential loneliness of limits of self, vision, health and ideas and the grace of the wisdom of the body and the mind in humility. In my case, this rescue fantasy is based on a vision of social transformation which in turn is held in place by an inner journey of survival, failure and resilience of experiences.

I try to create a sense of hope from the despairing dystopias that all of us carry within.

A critical reflection on pedagogy then to me is an authentic breakthrough in communication or a relationship to text. In this realm, experiences that posit as breakthrough may actually be closest to a breakdown or trauma. It is extremely difficult to find language and expression around them. Success seems to reside closest to failure. The difficulty in writing about pedagogy also stems from the complexity that writing always demands a selection—what are those pedagogic experiences, exchanges or encounters that the teacher decides to select, reflect and write about? The course of reflection is almost decided by the sheer act and moment of writing. There are multiple and contesting voices in the classroom that validate and reject the pedagogy practised by the teacher at the same moment. How does selection or exclusion of experiences based on the memory of experience/s with different students—the student who scored a high grade, the student who scored an average grade, the student who could not successfully pass the course or the student who dropped out of the course—shift the nature of the reflection on pedagogy? It is also the temporal and the socio-political context within which pedagogical exchange happens that shapes the pedagogy and reflection.

When does a teacher write about his or her pedagogy meaningfully? I understand that pedagogy itself has short term and long-term consequences. Then should its relevance only be assessed by short term pragmatic employability or by its long-term idealism and the social re-constructionist vision that it aspires to work towards? Most importantly, one is aware that listening in classroom involves interpersonal sharing and self-disclosure by students. This in turn poses the dilemma about ethics of writing around the pedagogic experience. The difficulty is due to the fact that the self-disclosure and interpersonal reflections in the classroom are also based on the trust of the setting, on students and colleagues and owe their emergence to the ethic of the collective whose reflection requires collective consent. The knowledge base of pedagogy is a shared living experience. This writing then for me is about being meditative about the discourse of teaching. I enter this space with humility which can sometimes be precarious and gentle. I also realize that at times my teaching like that of all others can rest on grandiose fantasies, which can be violent when they are oblivious of their limits.

What the term pedagogy does to me is what I would like to reflect about. There is a clear understanding that the being and self of the teacher is realized through the practice of teaching and learning. My struggle has always been to work through and work with the gaps between living and theorizing, reflecting on several experiences of meaningfulness and failure from several pedagogic moments of my classroom. Pedagogy and pedagogic reflections are like writing on the beach where a wave begins to approach, travel, and traverse and then it takes away the memory of the teacher's being, strivings and meanings in its receding flow back into the ocean. In all its simplicity, the essence of my pedagogy lies in the struggle to find a way of nurturing, planting and growing trees so that somebody else will enjoy their breeze in times to come. This is what I strive and work for. For me, good pedagogy revolves around the teacher becoming invisible and the memory of the entire classroom, texts or moments of relational understanding coming to comfort and provide the resilience to go on for the student even when the student is at the rock bottom facing the difficult challenges of her/ his life. This hope, this memory of care and reflection is what I strive for in my classroom as a teacher.

In the classroom spaces, one wonders about what one hopes and desires to teach and transact through the content. I try to work with pedagogy though three major axes: of content/ discipline and its epistemology. I work with a student-centred method of interacting and enabling the content in transaction and social reconstructionism is the goal. As I teach, I try to embody the ideals of some of my teachers who I value for academic rigour, academic freedom and social transformation. They have always inspired me in my engagement with the students. I carry my mentors in my thoughts. Here lies a secret desire that they witness what and how I teach and engage with the students in the classroom. There is this ego ideal in teaching, which is 'absent-present' a decisive evaluator mental imago, from where I reach certain ethics of my teaching and learning approach in the classroom. This leaves me with a thought—does one have to always be in a continuous search for a mentor who one respects, values and cherishes? The mentor as the ideal is perhaps sought less to validate one's teaching and more to have a continuous dialogue and reflection around the ideals and practices in one's own being. These mentors or teachers who I idealize act like an 'absent-present' conscience even as I strive to engage with the ideals and their practice in social transformation.

There is no single pedagogy, but there are pedagogies in action as students try to teach you through their experiences, struggles and challenges in any interaction in the classroom. Pedagogy is not just a teacher's ideas, being and practice but it actually evolves in the interaction, presence and absence of student(s) in the space called classroom. The classroom is a space, not a place, fluid in many contours created by the students and the teacher. The pedagogy and limits of the discipline also undergo a change when the playground, canteen, art gallery, seminar room and open arenas with blue skies and tall tress become a space for travelling and learning together.

Pedagogy is a collective cooperative experience where every moment is creative and intense, constructive and violent at the same time. I refer to violence also because classroom is a space for several sub-groups of identities and ideologies based on age, caste, class, sexualities, gender and abilities that clash and that there is a constant endeavour to learn, unlearn and relearn to create an environment of trust, care, respect and empathy. Classroom is a space full of contesting realities. Both the teacher and the students struggle to reach a shared and a critical understanding of the society they live in through their journeys in the classroom space. Intervention in the classroom challenges the everyday experience of the student and the teacher at home and the outside world. The pedagogy unsettles the existing hierarchies of self and the other in a continuous manner; there is a constant tension induced between the classroom and the outside world. As a teacher I recognize my role in negotiating this tension and also recognize how it helps me to validate and learn about my students' struggle between the university and the outside spaces.

As a teacher of Ambedkar University Delhi, I am constantly trying to engage with my pedagogic aims and objectives for providing quality education with equity and social justice. The classroom seating arrangement for most of my classes is a circle which I call as the 'circle of care' and we all sit to learn to listen and receive from each other. We try to move together through the texts and personal journeys to the inner worlds of students with their familial, socio-historical identities on psychological themes of childhood, exploration of identities, surviving failure, listening to the unpopular in the popular and surviving and listening to autobiographies. The study material is not just the scholarly articles and books, but also narratives of personal journeys. Experiences are treated as the most valuable and meaningful text in the classroom. We engage with complex themes of survival, resilience, pain, sexuality, child sexual abuse, neglect, inferiority around grades, and epistemic violence of the classmates in a competitive matrix. These serve as the context for texts to be chosen and reflected on. We learn to negotiate theory, text and the field through an intensive reflection of experiences based on every personal account in the classroom. The challenge in this pedagogy is about maintaining boundaries and regulating transferences between the teacher and the students, and also the entire group. Occasional self-disclosure on the part of the teacher may add to the relational dynamics at play in the classroom.

As we engage with social justice and equity we are also expected to innovate and create new pedagogies that question the existing hierarchy and hegemony and to enable the ideals to emerge gracefully and organically. In the process we are faced with the question of whether we are creating or constructing pedagogies. Creation is a primary process and the evolving structure is unknown while construction is based on an already existing template, one which is historically and culturally well-defined and which requires praxis in a pre-ordained manner. In creation, there are parts that are known and unknown, primarily in its exhilaration, struggle, passion, pain, rejection, deadness and survival. It is like the act of a child's play which is at once pleasurable, constructive, destructive and meaningful as it slowly moves to a discovery and exploring of new limits and possibilities.

Pedagogic freedom, self-reflexivity, humility and arrogance are all part of the daring attempt to dream to create a new episteme which Ambedkar University Delhi has provided me with. The social vision of Ambedkar and its social construction of reality in the classroom have always been a source of challenge as well as motivation to help me see limitations of my discipline and practice.

There has to be democracy and continuous dialogues across several aspects of pedagogy, curriculum and evaluation with the University's vision to make sense of limits of our pedagogic imagination and practice. This task when done by teachers' collective on a periodic basis would provide for critical imagination and engagement of pedagogues and their practices.

We need a community of professionals in a system that are not driven by competition but cooperation to work their way to a 'being mode' of life rather than 'having mode' of life and existence. To practise what we preach is to be open to the paradoxes in us as we struggle to negotiate the classroom with all the socio-cultural-historical struggle of identities. I am slowly trying to find a network of reflective practitioners who share the same world view to make sense of the struggle. This seeking of a community of professionals is to face the challenges of the socio-political onslaught and to build up the resilience as one engages with the complex realities of poverty and marginalities in the classroom. Being a teacher, pedagogy as praxis seems to help me survive several marginalizations of the self and the other.

The search for me is to carry meaningful memories that stay despite the turmoil in the outside world. This lingering effect provides a different tone to this note that I am writing now. And thus this writing is dedicated to all my academic institutions, mentors, students, colleagues, friends and my family who continue to help me in finding my identity as a teacher.

Section 2
Only Connect

When a person realizes he has been deeply heard, his eyes moisten. I think in some real sense he is weeping for joy. It is as though he were saying, 'Thank God Somebody heard me. Someone knows what it's like to be me.'

— Carl Rogers

Photo credit: Ananya Kushwaha

5

Only Connect

Some Reflections on Teaching

Usha Mudiganti

> Only connect the prose and the passion, and both will be exalted, and human love will be seen at its highest. Live in fragments no longer. Only connect, and the beast and the monk, robbed of isolation that is life to either, will die.
>
> —E.M. Forster. *Howards End* (1910)

I begin this 'paper' with a lot of trepidation. And from the moment I agreed to take up this challenge, I have wondered why I am so scared to talk about being a teacher, of believing that I sometimes succeed in making place for the 'life' of my students and of how that endeavour forms and re-forms my 'imagination of teaching'. I kept worrying till I recalled an incident. My teacher, Professor Hoshang Merchant, was invited by another of my teachers to share with her creative writing class his reasons for and process of writing poetry. A few minutes before his lecture was to begin, Professor Merchant confessed to being nervous about it. Until that moment, I had only known him as a very confident teacher who made poetry while teaching poetry in his classes. I said to him, 'But what is the worry, are you not reading out of your published essay

'How I write, Why I write'?[1]' He said, 'Yes, I am but don't you see that reading that to a bunch of strangers is like standing naked in public?' I persisted with, 'Sir, the kinds of things you say in your classes are way more radical than this essay.' His retort to that was the eye-opener. He calmly told me, 'You are my students, my children. I love you. Who are these children? Why should I stand naked in front of them?' Obviously, I did not have an answer to that. We walked into class early and found a nervous-looking young adult hovering near the door. Professor Merchant called him in and on confirming that he was a member of the creative writing class asked him what he wrote on. He blurted out sincerely, 'Fear'. Professor Merchant turned to me and said, 'Now I can talk to this class about how I write and why I write'.

I have recorded this entire anecdote here[2] because I learnt from it that one is able to speak about personal identities in public when the audience understands anxiety. I am a teacher. It is my professional identity but it is also one of those professions where the personal cannot be totally removed from the professional. And liberal arts classrooms are spaces where the most personal and intimate can and do become focal points for intense discussions while apart from the teacher, each student is aware that he/she inhabits a public space and is in a professional relationship with each other.

I have been attempting to execute this tight-rope walk for more than a decade now! In all these years, I have had many varieties of students, not just as regards their dreams and goals but also their world views. There is dramatic diversity in the experience of being a teacher and there will be much more diversity and drama to be lived out. Through all these changes till now, the one constant I have held on to is that

1. This was a condensed and an earlier version of two essays in his *The Man Who Would Be Queen* (2011), where it is divided into 'How I Write' and 'Why I Write' and he declares that he writes because it is 'a great liberation'. (Merchant, 2011, 154.)
2. Due permission has been taken from Professor Merchant to share this incident here.

I have to be a little more informed about the particular text we are engaging with in the class than my student would be. That is the one thing that I strive to keep constant through all these changes in the world around and within me. And the one learning is that as a teacher, I am working with live forces in the classroom. No student comes in a state of *tabula rasa* or is a container into whom knowledge can be poured. Students come into a programme and a class with aims, dreams, experiences, expectations and each of them also brings in many moods. And the teacher is trying to connect—connect the dots in her head to make a coherent picture, connect with each student who inhabits her personal world and while also inhabiting the space of the class. The teacher can hope, for the latter. A mere listing of all that each moment of teaching involves induces anxiety. And anxiety is a key term when one is talking of anything psychological.

I have had any number of conversations with my students, mostly girl-students and I have come to learn about issues that are bothering them psychologically. I have had girls talk of domestic difficulties and health issues (including mental health ones), girls hinting at hitting roadblocks in relationships and hoping that I would be able to clarify their thoughts, girls suddenly breaking down in class, and bright girls asking me whether they have the aptitude for literary studies. I have dealt with cases of girls coming back a few years after graduating to discuss life-choices, girls talking about the gap between idealistic classroom discussions and quotidian lives, a girl who spent two difficult hours with me to discuss the dissonance between her right leaning family and her inclination towards the left after getting radicalized in liberal arts classes, girls worrying about exploitative and sometimes abusive sexual relationships. I must have spent hours with these girls, mostly listening and trying to tell them that the issues raised were not crazy and that it was possible to find ways out of most situations. I do realize that these are moments when I am more of a mentor than someone with whom they work towards acquiring skills to find jobs. After all, my job is to lead discussions on literature and '[l]iterature, history, arts and ethics are but important means to a distinctly human end' (Hodges, 2002, 42). It should not be a surprise that there are moments when I am perceived to be a mentor to guide them into solutions that life throws up. The surprise was the realization that each time I am expected to share more than my interpretation of a literary text, I feel slightly anxious and display signs of resistance.

As the first step of towards working on this paper, I started looking for a text through which I could approach this issue. Serendipitously, I found my text in the form of an old greeting card, which literally fell out of some old papers. This card was given to me exactly a decade ago, by two students from an all-girls class I taught in my first full-time job at a college for girls from socially-disadvantaged family backgrounds. Until this card literally fell into my lap, I had completely forgotten about it. I still have no memory of those girls giving me this card. It is not the time-lapse between the event of receiving the card and this moment that can account for the lapse in memory. For I remember these very girls dancing in the college bus, during an excursion, to the tune of the latest hit-songs, completely oblivious to their hijabs falling off their heads and slipping off their shoulders too. I remember their telling me the recipes for various kinds of payasam in class when I tried to explain the difference between sugar and jaggery. Neither of those words were part of their active English vocabulary. They told me the words in Malayalam as ingredients in their recipes while I was teaching them English. I knew no Malayalam and they had very little English. I remember I started a contest with their class to see whether I learn Malayalam faster than their becoming functional in English. In case you are interested in the result of the contest, it became the proverbial hare and tortoise race where I was the hare. I remember drawing a horse on the board in the first class with them to make them recognize the word I had uttered. In that instance my Indian version of Received Pronunciation of English was the added obstacle to their comprehension. If I have such clear memories of all these events, how and why did I blank out this card? The little I know of psychoanalysis tells me that this is a clear case of trauma. I was traumatized by the card. What does the card say which made me repress the memory? It was a regular new year card on which one of the girls wrote that I as the teacher had brought with me 'exotic colours and filled our life with joy and love'. I think that was too much to bear for me. All along I had thought I was teaching English. And that I was struggling to share my interpretation of Andrew Marvell's *To His Coy Mistress* and Henrik Ibsen's *'A Doll's House'* to girls who had to come to college in uniforms which included a properly pinned up hijab for the Muslim girls. And I was myself following a dress-code to hold on to that much-needed job—donning a sari each morning, which ostensibly made me look like a 'respectable person', a teacher. I thought I was struggling with these dichotomies and difficulties each day.[3] Never did I imagine that I was perceived as someone using exotic colours to fill lives with joy and love. All I know was that I was struggling to connect with them. A decade later, I am still struggling to connect with my students. In the process, I suppose I do make some small dents in lives, but I am surer of my experience of the feelings held by my students. Through some of the worst times of my life, the mere thought that I have to stand up and speak to a group of keen young minds has made me discipline my thought-process into logic and coherence; it has helped me keep my sanity. Through these years of struggles in literature classrooms, I am nowhere close to feeling that I have connected. However, I have understood the desperation in the poignant phrase—'only connect!'

References

Braithwaite, E.R. *To Sir, With Love*. (1959). New York: Jove Books.

Hodges, Louis W. Applied Professional Ethics as an Academic Subject in the Humanities. In K.C. Baral (Ed.) *Humanities and Pedagogy: Teaching of Humanities Today* (pp. 37-42). Delhi: Pencraft International.

Merchant, Hoshang. How I Write. Why I Write. In *The Man Who Would be Queen* (2011). New Delhi: Penguin.

3. I am aware that they were nowhere close to the ones recorded by E.R. Braithwaite in *To Sir, With Love* (1959) or many others who have worked with students from socially disadvantaged groups.

6

Churning of the Ocean of Learning

Lessons and Gifts from a Journey with My Students

Amit Singh

Riverbank plum-tree
Do your reflected blossoms
Really flow away?

A serendipitous reading of this beautiful haiku by Buson struck me instantaneously as a metaphor for teacher-student relationship and the larger ecosystem of educational institutions. I see the 'plum-tree' here as an image of institutions of learning and knowledge, the 'blossoms' as teachers and their interactions with students, and the streams that 'flow away' clearly as students' life journeys. I often wonder how much of what I teach becomes part of my students' lives. Am I just an individual with some legitimate power to help them attain some credentials in the form of degrees and grades, or do I have a little more agency than that? If the latter, in what ways do students carry the 'reflections' of my interactions with them in their journeys ahead? This anxiety, I think, is one of the chief driving forces behind the little pedagogical experiments that I attempt in my classrooms.

I think, as a teacher, many of us aspire to get the best of our students' inner expressions. That is also my touchstone of being someone's true well-wisher. Quite a few times I have realized that we as teachers are utter failures in recognizing the dreams and aspirations of our students. I will cite an example to illustrate this. In the very first year of my formal teaching, one of my literature students in the final year, an absolutely irregular and incredibly careless 'low-performer' with whom I had struck some kind of friendship, gifted me a book titled *Servants of Sahib* (1923), with the following words, 'you cannot say no to this gift as this is the first book written in English in Ladakh, the place from where I come. You cannot say no, also, for the reason that it was written by my great-grandfather. Please do not mind the numerous spelling mistakes and grammatical errors in this book. It is much more than what can simply be read.' Later he told me that he chose English Literature as his subject because he saw it as a legacy passed down to him by his great-grandfather.

I really feel that when we as teachers are not able to understand the aspirations of such students, we are nothing but failures. It was sad that he conveyed his history to his teacher at the fag end of his BA Honours. But it was also significant that he shared these words and that book with me because prior to that I had given him the application form for Jawaharlal Nehru Univeristy (JNU) MA entrance examination—an act that must have symbolized in his mind my faith in his intelligence and knowledge. Quite early in my career, this quiet Ladakhi student taught me how time is irretrievably lost when teachers judge their students on grounds merely defined by regularity, refined speech and flawless writing. In that process, we automatically strain out those students who may lack the cultural capital and the motivation to interact with teachers and their peers simply because they are different. This experience has guided me in my career so far in paying attention to the silent, low-key, reluctant ones in class whom I have always found full of intellectual energy, utmost sincerity and a rare awe for knowledge.

I have continually noticed in my class interactions the need for constant vigil over various negotiations that our students grapple with in the outside world. We should never fall into the trap of considering a student's university days as comprising a unidirectional and singular world; we must realize that every student engages simultaneously with multiple 'worlds' both inside and outside the campus. I feel that this fact must inform all our classroom transactions, especially the assessment situations. I believe that an assessment ought to get the best out of our students' learning. It should not be a formality that may help them attain some grades. Quite often in our zeal to extract better academic performance from our students, i.e. making them attain highest possible grades comprising highly praiseworthy credentials, especially in case of our research students, we seldom remember the psychological background and the conflicting 'worlds' in which our students live. Such an understanding is no doubt difficult, but being aware of possible clashes between the several worlds of the student perhaps equips us in better ways, say while transacting with our students in situations of crisis that they might not be even willing to share with anyone. Allow me a little digression, but this caution is needed in all our relationships. How often a casual routine call by a roommate or a colleague, that later turns out to be an emergency call, is ignored by us as a quotidian reality of our stressful lives? We forget that just a minute or so long chat over the phone was all that the caller expected at that precise moment. We also forget how important we can be for others, in their moments of crisis at least. Do we not all need, many a time, a patient listener and a companion who would prefer not to judge us? How many times have we realized this in our interactions with our friends and family? Have we not hung up our phones by saying that, "I am busy right now"? We miss to notice the urgency or desperation in the tone of an otherwise very calm caller. I recall that after weeks of intense hard work at the last stage of her submissions, one of my MA Dissertation students started feeling fatigued. Of course, she never complained about anything and kept on meeting my demands for revised versions of her final draft. Sometimes, even a small typing error was taken very seriously by me. Needless to say that missing any significant point in a presentation was a complete no. In short, a perfect and meticulous draft was my minimum demand. While these demands would be justified from the academic standpoint, I cannot absolve myself of blame for my inability to understand, the psychological background of that scholar and for what happened thereafter. Although submission on time and successful defense was the ultimate result of the aforementioned student's dissertation, this is just one part of the story. The other part perhaps became one of the most intense moments for me as a teacher, an experience that informed my insights into the necessity of understanding the mental state of my students. I must confess that a week or so after this student of mine was through with her dissertation, she had to be hospitalized. She temporarily lost her vision, and developed other complications. After a day or so, she was diagnosed with multiple sclerosis and a series of mental and physical struggles began for her. I felt guilty about failing to recognize the mental and physical stress she was under, all along. I have to record that she dealt with, and is still dealing with, her condition in the most positive manner. We are still in touch with each other, and our meetings and gatherings sometimes revolve around her experience as a schoolteacher when she tells me how she tries to understand the 'why?' behind every 'what?' associated with her students. This experience has made me realize the necessity to engage with psyche of students, at least on the occasions in which they feel threatened in whatever ways and to whatever degrees. I am more confident now to understand my students better and approach them more openly. I do not know for what reasons, but now I feel more confident about apologizing to my students in case of need. I think this student of mine stands apart amongst my most influential counsels.

So far I have been speaking about experiences that I recall as significant yet not so happy. Let me also share that some of my happiest moments have been those spent in the classroom, albeit not on occasions when I was strategically trying to tackle the 'shortcomings' of my students. There were occasions, too, when I felt that I drastically failed; I failed when I imposed on myself the need to maintain distance from some of my students. I wish I were a little more confident in understanding their desires, dreams and aspirations, rather than simply distancing myself from them, despite my innate potential to stand alongside them.

As a teacher, I think, we must aspire to overcome monotonous ways of showing off before students. My experiences have made me more confident to move in that direction and be honest with my students. I strongly believe, that as teachers, our complete control over class transactions is nothing but a displaced extension of our knowledge and research from which our students are seldom able to create their own knowledge base. I feel that we are impressed by students and we also try to impress them through eloquence in speech sprinkled with whatever we can recall or repackage from our knowledge base, skipping the vast treasures emanating from our experiences beyond bookish scholarship. I am not denying the necessity for teachers to be knowledgeable. In fact, I believe that there is no substitute to scholarship and knowledge in teaching. However, I feel that scholarship has to be genuine and erudite. Not the strategic show-off of google-search and from-my-notes kind of 'scholarship'. This applies to the genuine use of speech too, rather than the easily attainable mastery of languages adopted by demagogues. If I can speak for my own discipline, i.e. literature, we redeem ourselves from being mere degraded sophists. I feel in almost all cases, eloquence in speech is a matter of cultural capital that the majority of us do not possess. So, in my classes, I categorically refuse to accept the 'charm' of eloquence in English alone. I explain the need to master the medium of our expression though. However, it is developing skills in our own languages and dialects for which I constantly motivate my students. This also helps me to motivate my students for further investigations into knowledge traditions through tales, proverbs, riddles, jokes, and even texts. While this pedagogical shift allows my students to actively participate in creating methodology of class interactions where they too bring in texts and facilitate discussions. This also moves the class discussions beyond the confines of expressions based solely on English language.

One of the regular experiments in all my courses is to have about twenty percent of my assessments based on ten to twenty questions that each student submits at the end of the semester. This gives us a shared question bank of about five hundred questions for each paper I teach. In fact, I myself begin with a question, which is basically a trick question; I ask my students to share with me the names of their favourite authors, poets, thinkers, activists, etc. After a few names have poured in, I ask them to name one book that their respective favourites liked reading. Students find it fascinating to find out which books Freud and Marx were got to read. Anyway, the process of framing questions for a question bank that will be discussed in class motivates students to start thinking in terms of asking questions rather than giving answers. Although this experiment needs to be made more effective, I have been getting interesting and original questions from my students, that, too, without any anxiety to arrive at the right answers. Along with these experiments, I feel engaging students in seminars and conferences gives them immense confidence and exposure. Over the past two years, I have seen transformations in my students after their return from American Folklore Society's annual conferences. This I submit could be reckoned as one of my significant achievements beyond the classroom.

I wish and hope that my students will remain connected with each other. This certainly will help them to feel stronger and confident. This is what is amiss in our lives too. I feel our students need to learn to appreciate others. I also feel that this conviction will help them in maintaining honesty in all their relationships. I think these little cautions have helped me as a teacher and have reinforced my conviction in honesty in teacher-taught relationship. It has, also helped me to think over my actions in this capacity and ask repeatedly if any of my decisions crosses the thin line between being strict and being vindictive towards my students. This caution has made me feel proud and content. It also makes me feel influential in the lives of my students, the streams through which my reflected blossoms perhaps flow away.

7

Reaching Out-Reaching Within

Reflections of a Young Teacher

Devika Sharma

Two years ago, one of my colleagues asked me: What do you feel is the difference between teaching children of primary classes (I taught primary classes for some years) and those in higher education? That was asked two years ago when I was about to step into teaching at the university level. Now, with one batch of students graduating with their master's degree and having been the Programme Coordinator for two years, which amongst many things also means coming across many issues related to students' lives, I have had the privilege to become a small part of their lives and getting to know possibly what it means to be a student in higher education. The question that was put to me two years ago has been with me and I have reflected on it. Of many things, I have come to realize that students reach higher education with an accumulated sense of pain, the pain of not being heard, and not understood. As the system is the same, all are affected!

As an aside, I would like to share a small incident that reminded and reassured me of the necessity to be with the person's whole being. Interventions on an everyday basis are important for one to function, but they are quite invisible and may not form part of the discourse. Some days back, my son and his cousin were playing in the room where I was reading a book. Children were all over the bed, and their toys were all over the room. I am quite used to all the mess and noise and the book was quite interesting. Both the children were playing and it was kind of aggressive. I would look up from the book in between to make sure no one was hurt. That day my nephew seemed unusually aggressive in his comments or gestures—he wanted to hurt his cousin and he was quite vocal about it. As their play went on, I began feeling uncomfortable. So, I thought of asking him how the day at school had gone off, because as a primary class teacher I used to find it a site of strife, disturbance and difficulties. He answered in monosyllables. There was nothing that seemed worth noting at that moment, I felt! I then asked about his home. He said he had a fight with his sister. I heard his singular statement and observed his expressions. He is not a very articulate child. After that brief talk, he was different with his cousin. The game was still aggressive but there was playfulness. In fact, after that I could sleep off and when I woke up I found both of them silently playing on their own. It left me wondering how we as people at times do not want resolution but wish to be heard, however insignificant it may sound to others. And there is such a need to have someone in life who would listen to our commonplace rumblings.

In higher education, students have more sophisticated means than earlier to make sense of the world, but more than that, I feel they have learnt to articulate much more than when they were younger. But our cultural, social and educational system is such that we do not give space to articulate what they feel or think about. I remember most of my students in Classes II, III and even V when told to write about 'My Mother' would write accounts, having similar content as though there is a universal mother and the paragraph typically ended with 'I love my mother' (I am sure we all do but what about other feelings?). I wondered how no one wrote about how they felt when their mothers went out to work leaving them alone waiting or when they had to have food that they did not wish to, or when they were stopped from doing what gave them pleasure, what did they exactly like about their mother, etc. It is just to say that from childhood we learn to not own our experiences and words, and we quickly learn to betray our feelings despite acquiring progressively larger vocabularies.

I would like to share one more anecdote to draw our attention to the need to listen to our students. One day, around 3:30 pm one student came to me in my cubicle looking for her friend. The friend had reached out to me several times in the weeks that had passed but somehow we could not manage to find a suitable time for the meeting for various reasons. Before the student left, I asked her to give me a call once she found her friend. After an hour or so when I thought of leaving the campus, I called up the student. I was in panic when she told me her friend was found unconscious and they were in some room taking care of her. After a couple of minutes, I also reached the room. The room was glum with five-six girls huddled together. I had come to listen to one person, but here there were three or four among them who looked distressed. One of the students (it was not the one who had fallen unconscious) was inconsolable. She had been rebuked for not delivering what was expected of her in completing her dissertation. Many times, I feel we fail to recognize how the lack of competency in English language compromises one's writing and that writing is also a way of thinking. The problem of not completing the dissertation in the manner it was expected was posited as her individual problem. The site of the problem may be located in the person but sometimes it needs to be and can be helped if it is placed outside at a systemic level, for it can then address the issue at large. We appreciate hard work in our education system, and students from difficult circumstances are left with only their labour to make a mark in our English medium semester mode system. Two years is a rather inadequate period time to acquire and be part of the finesse that we euologize in the university. I have wondered about the word excellence. It has perplexed me. In excellence, I feel is hidden loneliness, away from the ordinariness and smallness. As this student was being consoled by two others in the room, I listened to the student who had wanted to talk with me. As I heard her, I was quite aware of the student who had come to me an hour or so earlier sitting nearby. She looked distraught. She had a story to tell, but my body language did not help her. I was too conscious of the time, as reaching my son waiting for me at home was weighing heavily on my mind. When I came out of the room, I felt strange. I could not cry. I could not explain to myself as to how I was feeling. So much work was there that needed to be done beyond achieving excellence!

In the past two years I heard a number of personal stories around making career options, diseases, family discord, rape, sexual abuse, molestation, death and loss. Most of them were speaking for the first time. I have reflected over the matter if it would help to start a small group in the School where we can read texts (poems, songs, stories, articles, novels etc) watch movies, listen to songs related to issues of loss, abuse, sexuality, identity and so on and talk about and share our experiences. I do not want it to be a course and bound by marks, competition, and display of competencies. It has to do with just listening to ourselves!

I have my limits when I listen. I know I tend to support someone or the other even before a person has spoken. I dread listening to stories of difficult pasts. I also wonder whether there is a voyeur in me who wants to know others' secrets. Sometimes, I can sense lies, but I let them come out because it is not easy to reveal the truth and hear the truth. I also understand that many events occurred before and after the actual event that one struggles to make sense of and articulate around. As I listen sometimes I am not able to suspend my immediate worries—that I have a child who is waiting for me, that I need to prepare for the class scheduled for the following day, or that some work would get postponed and nobody in the office would understand my situation and as to how these stories would affect my well-being. I also have found myself worrying about the students in conflict with other colleagues. Sometimes I feel their 'come on, get on with life' attitude has also helped some students. Some of the dilemmas after listening to the students are whether I should share those inputs with the rest of the faculty who are either teaching the students currently or are going to teach them in the semester/s to follow.

And what should be shared and how? Should there be a forum within the School to address such issues? I want to protect such a student from becoming a 'case'. But at the same time, how do we address course requirements—attendance, assessment situations, deadlines, and gradings.

I am not formally trained in listening. So, as an immediate response I talk about *ehsaas* the psychotherapy and counselling unit at Ambedkar University Delhi to the students who want to share their difficult journeys with me. I have also wondered whether I am giving away my agency as a teacher to *ehsaas* too quickly. I also wonder if I have begun to feel that my responsibility is till I take the student to *ehsaas* or has the space *ehsaas* occupied my mind and taken away my agency to be with the student? Many a time, I have felt guilty. The student trusted me to share with me his/her life story and I redirected him/her to a new place (which is a more professional space!). I have not experienced what it means to sit on the couch, what it means to negotiate the fee in a low-fee clinic, and how different is the practise of counselling there from other clinics? I have also felt uncomfortable asking about how their experience was in *ehsaas*. After the student has approached *ehsaas*, I do not know how the student is doing—whether I should approach the student or the clinic or should I even bother to find out. In some cases, I have felt that the student needed more than just *ehsaas*—networks for legal action as well as a safe and protected space for stay.

i reach out
and
i reach within

8

Understanding Learners in My Language Classroom

Monishita Hajra Pande

I teach English language courses to first year undergraduate students and specifically to students with basic to lower intermediate proficiency in English. In my classroom, affect plays a very important role as most of my learners view English as a language that they need to master in order to fulfil their ambitions and dreams; to them, it is a language that can help them to achieve upward social mobility and change people's perceptions about them. Not being proficient in English for them is a social stigma that they deal with in their everyday interactions within and outside the university space. Moreover, as AUD is a university where English is the medium of instruction, it becomes essential for students to improve their overall English language proficiency in order to do well academically and blend socially. The majority of students come into the course with feelings of fear, anxiety, nervousness or shame.

To be able to develop their language proficiency, it is imperative to get them talking in the classroom in English. Therefore, addressing their feelings is the first step to making them comfortable in the classroom. Most of my learners have shared that they feel judged by people because of their poor proficiency in English. As a result, many of them choose to remain silent in the class because they are scared of making mistakes.

For a language classroom to be acquisition-rich, it is important to encourage meaningful interaction in the target language (Walsh 2006), which is possible only when learners 'open up', and feel comfortable to use the language. Creating a non-threatening and non-judgemental space then becomes the key to a communicative classroom.

Krashen (1987) proposes the affective filter hypothesis, which claims that several affective variables are at play in a second language classroom, which can have an impact on language learning. In other words, when students feel anxious, nervous or have low self-esteem, their affective filter is 'high' which impedes acquisition of second language in the classroom. Therefore, making students emotionally comfortable is an important step to initiate the process of learning.

Research in the area of Second Language Acquisition (SLA) suggests that focusing too much on language form (grammar and structures) and less on meaning inhibits language learning and acquisition (Norris & Ortega 2001). This assumption translates into reassuring my learners that they are not expected to speak flawless English and that making mistakes is part of the learning process; this allows me to get my learners to speak and write in a language that they are not comfortable using.

A language teacher has the advantage of using any content in her classroom, as a language is both the means as well as the end. I often choose activities that are based on themes or topics which evoke genuine feelings and which are context-sensitive. I believe that feelings play an important role in making communication authentic.

I have observed that my students bring in lived experiences related to various social issues that we discuss in our classes. Whether it be gender or caste discrimination, child labour, child marriage, dowry system, female foeticide or poverty, they have experienced some or all of these very closely. In order to allow them to express their anxieties and experiences (while using English), I get my learners (elementary or basic users of English) to work on poster presentations.

As part of this activity, students get into pairs and choose a social problem or issue that directly affects their lives and prepare a poster in which they can draw, paint, paste or do anything to express their thoughts along with some written material in English (they get enough time to research and put down some written words in English). They are then asked to present the poster to the entire class and talk about the problem in greater detail: personalizing it, problematizing it, and raising questions and solutions which are often elusive with no easy answers. This exploration has been humbling for me as a teacher as I get to learn immensely when students share, open-up and engage in questions that affect all of us –directly or indirectly. Students share their struggles in addressing these social issues and describe their personal journeys in resisting social evils such as early marriage, dowry, and child labour for instance. Their stories get unfolded in the classroom where they end up using English to talk about the experiences that are very close to their immediate lives.

Students share how they have to struggle to earn their living while attending university classes. Female students talk about their struggle to resist marriage and reach higher education while many male students also share how they try to support their mothers, sisters or girlfriends to pursue their dreams and speak against traditions, which are patriarchal and orthodox.

Many a time, my learners come back to me in their second or third year of undergraduate studies and recall their experiences in the English language classroom. Here are some of their comments, which reinforce my belief that creating an inclusive space in the classroom that is non-threatening, non-judgemental and less performance-driven facilitates learning and working positively towards strengthening learner motivation. Students need constant assurance that they can cross the language barrier and that it is possible.

> I was always a backbencher in my school but in English class, I got a chance to sit in the front row and I started believing that I too have ideas. (Lakshay Gaurav, Mathematics)

> I had thought I would leave AUD after my first two weeks of college. I felt that I know nothing, I cannot even speak English and others are so good. But EPC class made me believe that English can be learnt without feeling conscious and ashamed. (Gunjan Sharma, Psychology)

The majority of language teachers complain that students with basic or elementary proficiency in English are reticent in classrooms and do not participate in activities; I have also heard teachers expressing their concerns over low attendance and lack of punctuality amongst students which undoubtedly become a serious hurdle in maintaining continuity in classroom activities and tasks. I too face such challenges, but I have come to realize that engaging students in dynamic classroom interactions, creating a positive learning environment and making space for emotions and affect play an important role to reduce learner reticence and increase learner motivation.

Whenever a student misses a class or fails to reach on time, I try to understand the reason behind these failures and often I find myself connecting with their everyday struggles. Most of the times, the reasons are genuine and allow me to peep into their everyday challenges and issues. I must also admit that in some cases, on the surface the reason may seem to be sheer lack of motivation and disinterest in academics; however, when I probe further to understand the reason for low motivation, I get surprised as to how we again tread on areas of their lives and experiences which are disturbing and are connected to the social realities that they are surrounded with. For instance, I had a student who was always late to class. Despite repeated reminders and pointing out that it was not acceptable, he failed to come to class on time. One day I decided to spend time with him to understand the reason as I trusted his words 'ma'am, I try a lot to come on time but I fail'.

Interestingly, he opened up to me and shared his daily routine and that he needs to run a shop to support his family after the bereavement of his father. He talked about his three sisters who are struggling to continue their studies at school, as they have to work as domestic helps to support their basic needs and his ailing mother who tries to take care of the shop while he attends classes. That conversation made me believe that we as teachers can easily blame students and speak from a moral high ground about punctuality and attendance, but the realities that our students face are often distanced from our own understanding of expectations and situations. After our conversation, I found this student in class on time; perhaps, he had also managed to negotiate with his struggles to some extent after our interaction.

As I am an English language teacher, I also need to ensure that the target language is being learnt (English) while I acknowledge that feelings and emotions are important. In this context, arises the question of the use of the mother tongue in language classroom. One will have to deal with how much of it can be used, why use it and other related questions. On the one hand, it is important to maximize the use of the target language in the classroom, but on the other hand, judicious use of the learner's first language can not only play an important role in developing language proficiency but also adequately address learner anxiety and nervousness.

Building a positive rapport with learners is an important aspect and I often use Hindi to facilitate rapport building. I encourage them to use English in the classroom and during activities we try to help each other to express in English as that is the main aim of the course: to be able to communicate in English. However, there is always room to interact in Hindi to express their feelings about the course, university life, and discuss questions, doubts and anxieties. I have found that focusing on what they wish to say rather than how they say it, helps me to connect with my learners.

Sharing authority and power with learners also helps to reduce learner anxiety and gives them more freedom. The teacher decides the course content, methodology and assessment, but it is possible to infuse a spirit of mutual decision-making and sharing responsibilities with learners in day-to-day teaching.

I believe that authority and power in the classroom need to remain fluid and dynamic; sharing them with learners also promotes learner autonomy and motivates them to take responsibility for their own learning. Activities, which encourage self-learning and research, play an important role in creating a more democratic classroom space. Peer review and feedback also allow learners to value each other's comments and insights and move towards independent learning. These conscious strategies infuse confidence in my learners and they begin to realize that they have immense potential to direct their learning and lives.

I think engaging with knowledge is an activity which not only involves cognitive processes but also activates our affective dimension. To make knowledge relevant, one has to connect learning to learners' everyday experiences and to motivate and sustain authentic communication and meaningful interactions in the class, affect plays a central role in the teaching and learning process. It is important to open up the classroom space for learners to jointly participate in the process of meaning making and learn from each other's experiences; this in turn creates a healthy learning environment, which is engaging, productive and enriching for both teachers and learners.

References

Krashen, S.D. (1987). *Principles and Practice in Second Language Acquisition.* New Jersey: Prentice-Hall International.

Walsh, S. (2006). *Investigating Classroom Discourse.* London: Routledge.

Norris, J. and Ortega, L. (2001). Does type of instruction make a difference? Substantive findings from a meta-analytic review in *Language Learning* 51(1): 157-213.

9

Toys and Teachers

Deepti Sachdev

They do not make them
like they used to,
easy
to pull apart
and put back together again.

Those illusions
of control over toys
and
surrender to teachers.

The joys of a mess, well made,
and the triumphs
of order
slowly earned.

My toys and my teachers
have taught me much, the
pleasures of play,
the pains of pedantry.

My moments,
my memories,
my wastes my wants,
my silent companions,
my violent ideals.

They broke me,
and put me back,
together again.
So I can break myself,
and put myself back,
together again.

And hence, it is,
I wonder,
if tact and technology
would ever make
for good teachers and toys.

Section 3
Of Teachers and Students

It is better to withhold
Than to fill to overflowing
It is better to refrain
Than to push to the extreme

— Lao Tsze

Photo credit: Shyam B. Menon

10

Engaging Beyond Surface

The Interplay of Cognition and Affect

Richa Awasthy

My interaction with my students...

I find it hard to call myself a teacher because the conventional meaning of a teacher is 'someone knowledgeable and one who imparts knowledge to students.' I do not think I know so much. My guiding force in teaching has been to enter the class with broad objectives, to work through diversions and to take a multi-route tributary to arrive at my point. This happens mainly due to the space created in a classroom for discussion and deliberation.

What does it mean to me to be a teacher? When did I become one? I often wonder about this. Is my role one of teaching or mentoring and facilitating the learning process? I feel being a teacher encompasses all of this. In other words, being a teacher means becoming instrumental in the holistic development of one's students.

Many times, opportunities arise when a teacher gets to interact with her students on issues other than course content. My account is along similar lines.

I teach a course on Organizational Behaviour to MBA students where self and interpersonal issues are discussed. Some students meet me beyond the classroom context to discuss their personal matters, life challenges and difficulties in managing interactions. While reflecting on my interactions with my students I have come to observe the following trends:

Open Mindset

I make an attempt to enter the classroom with an open mind and consider my students as participants and cofacilitators in classes/sessions. Thus my sessions are perceived as being very interactive. In many of my sessions, I accept my ignorance with respect to certain issues and later after working further; I return back to the class with newer thoughts and perspectives.

There have been instances when students have shared things against my values and morals. In such instances, despite our differences in perception, I have tried to listen and help the students deal with their feelings.

A girl shared with me that she had sex with her boyfriend and now she was feeling very guilty. A genuine understanding of her feelings helped me to look beyond my value system. Without making any judgemental or prescriptive statement, I listened to her patiently.

Reflective Questions

I try to raise reflective questions in class discussions, especially in electives so that the participants are able to derive lessons from their personal life experiences. This helps to actively involve participants in the meaning-making process.

My favourite reflective questions are: 'What did you do well in that situation?'; 'How do you prefer to learn?'

Such reflective questions help participants to establish a connection with the topic under discussion. Reflection helps to promote deeper learning by looking at situations through an expansive and ever-evolving lens and by asking oneself searching questions that challenge one's assumptions about the world and self. Further, it gives me an opportunity to get into the world of my students.

One day a boy got upset in my Transactional Analysis class. I was sharing my life experiences and giving many examples to explain various ego states. He was reminded of his relation with his mother. I could sense his disturbance. However I decided not to intrude and wait till he spoke to me himself. After the class he shared that, 'My mother used to leave me at the gate and I felt very angry with my mother...' Our conversations continued thereafter.

Developmental Relationship

The kinds of human problems that bring students to me revolve around difficulties in intergroup adjustment, lack of assertiveness, low confidence and so on.

A boy was a fresher in terms of having no experience of working in organizations. He was an introvert and had good writing skills. After spending two months in the MBA programme, one day he met me in my office. He was finding it difficult to work in the team which he was a part of. He was very hardworking and always willing to take up work on behalf of other team members. Gradually, he developed the feeling of being used by classmates. Being an introvert he had only two friends. I listened to him patiently and explored the possibilities of managing teamwork dynamics. I raised questions which made him see how he was impacting his team mates. This helped him understand the situation better. Gradually, he became confident and could handle team dynamics differently.

Empathetic Listening

There have been moments when I did not have any solution to offer, yet I tried to listen empathetically. In these moments I particularly felt that trust was very important for the development of the relationship. To share an instance, let me talk about a student's situation which was very challenging to handle. This journey with the student was also full of potential.

My student had a strained relationship with his father. He was feeling guilty about his behaviour towards his father. On the other hand, he also had a lot of anger vis-à-vis his father. Through our regular dialogue we realized that it was difficult for him to just 'forgive and forget'. It took him more than a year to feel better. Then he started feeling the need for bringing his relationship with his father to a neutral level, where they could at least talk. Instead of criticizing his father, he started thinking about his father's perspective.

Another student (who used to talk often with me about his personal life) was very hesitant to share that he was attracted towards men. I said, 'It is okay and my feelings towards you have not changed due to your sharing this with me'. Then I went on to ask him, 'Why did you feel, I would not be comfortable with this reality of yours?' He replied, 'I had thought that as you are religious, do meditation and seem to be spiritual, so you would not accept me'. His statement was a revelation to me... how people interpret our overt behaviour or how he was interpreting my behaviour for that matter!

Philosophy of 3Ps

Perceptivity, passion and person: I feel it is important for a teacher to enjoy interaction with participants and consider them as experienced people. Participants in our classes bring their life experiences to the classroom for discussion. It is important for a teacher to act as a facilitator

Traditionally, education has looked at the outcomes of classroom discussions in terms of cognitive learning. In this process, the affective and emotional aspects of the student's life are neglected. On the contrary, I feel that pedagogy should offer space for both cognitive and affective dimensions. However, the roles of thinking, feeling and reflecting/intuiting are complementary within this process.

My overall journey as a teacher can be summed up as that of a facilitator. Learning plays a very important role in an individual's life. Learning is not only a source of generating livelihood but is also an enabler of making life more meaningful. It is generally accepted that learning can take many different forms and can be acquired using different tools. This has been a guiding force and has given me the courage to experiment with in the classroom and keep my sessions interactive and reflective. Overall teaching would help students to construct their own knowledge through their experiences. We need to treat our student participants as active members in the classroom. Hence teaching should be 'learner-centric'.

Conclusion

My experience with students has made me realize that teaching involves going beyond the curriculum. It is the interplay of affect and cognition. Undoubtedly, subject knowledge is important; however emotional connection with students is equally crucial. My interactions with my students make me feel worthy as a human being. Teaching is a learning experience for me too. I genuinely feel indebted to my students for sharing some aspects of their lives and in the process I too have learnt, evolved and transformed as a person.

11
Learning from Teaching

Gunjan Sharma

I began teaching at Ambedkar University Delhi (AUD) as a faculty member in the School of Education Studies, in 2011. I was a fresh graduate of Master's of Education programme and prior to that I had completed all the requirements of becoming a schoolteacher. While I initially aspired to work in the public school system, as I pursued my doctoral degree, the idea of working in a university started to appeal more and more to me. The academic autonomy in teaching and the space for study and research that a university position provides, motivated me to join AUD when I had such an opportunity. All this while, my experience of university teaching and research has reinforced my decision.

Having been a student of education, at the time, I began teaching, I was familiar with the theory and ideas that inform teaching-learning. The perspectives of critical pedagogy and education for critical inquiry in particular inspired me (Apple 2009). However, the experience of teaching at the postgraduate level, made me revisit what I thought I knew. It also made me reflect on the differences in the application of what I knew to higher education—particularly in the current socio-political contexts of adult learners. In the process of learning and improving my practice, I erred on several occasions.

I recognized early on that postgraduate students bring deep-rooted assumptions about the social world to the classroom. These assumptions are sometimes clearly articulated and sometimes reflected in classroom discussions. I now also understand that these are early indications of the theoretical trajectory(/ies) that may appeal to a student. As I began teaching, I saw some of these commonsense notions as 'problems'. I spent considerable time to prepare myself to solve and address these immediately. I thereby missed on several opportunities to engage in and facilitate a dialogue. The classroom discussions were often dominated by the students who had the ability to speak in 'politically correct' fashion. The efforts at encouraging others to speak did not work.

I also began with the assumption that learners in a postgraduate classroom would generally keep themselves informed about the socio-political developments around them. I sometimes based my classroom presentations and lectures around these cases and instances. As a result, I often spent a substantial amount of class-time on informing the students, talking much more than planned, and unintentionally closing the space for discussion around the subject matter in question in the given time of a lecture.

It took me considerable time in understanding how to explain the purpose of the assessments to the students for the courses that I taught. The intended aim of most of my assessments was to enable skills of analysis and problem-solving in a contextual fashion. However, the location of the reading material in these assessments was not always very well thought out. I assumed that students would draw connections between what they read and their observations without much mediation on my part as this was observed by them in the classroom presentations. This also stemmed from a substantial difference in my previous experience of assessment and the assessment practices at AUD as compared to that of the students.

In the process of thinking about my practice, talking with students and colleagues with longer experience, I have been able to strike a balance in most of these areas that I explicitly identified. Student feedback has been the most valuable in helping me understanding my practice. On most of the occasions, the feedback given by the students in informal interactions, rather than the written anonymous feedback that they submit at the end of the courses, has been much more candid and elaborate. These interactions with students have also enabled me to relate to the students better and seemingly also provided them space to assess my practice and inform me.

There are other aspects of my practice on which I am still working.

One of these is developing the ability to understand the diverse and many a time not so well articulated motivations of students for attending a programme of study. I admit that I have not always been able to comprehend the outcomes that a student expects from a course and programme in general. While I appreciate that these expectations may not be clearly framed, even a general understanding of what a student may be looking for in a course or why a student is making certain choices helps in framing class discussions more meaningfully. I have been working to find ways to make sense of the gap between my intentions of teaching and students' intent of learning. I have also been fascinated to find a growing body of literature on this issue that indicates that a fairly large number of higher education faculty members share these experiences (Trigwell, Posser & Taylor 1994)

I am still trying to find a balance between being accommodative and flexible with and yet ensuring discipline of time among students. I have learnt vicariously that how one balances these two axes, has an impact not only on the rapport that teachers and students share but also on the group dynamics among the students.

In the process of navigating through these experiences, I have learnt in substantive ways about teaching in the higher education context.

One of these learnings, relates to the idea of teaching itself. The meaning of teaching has been debated in educational theory ever since the inception of the field (Carr 2003). On the one hand, it is understood as 'never more than a means' that has no point and purpose except the activities to which it introduces students (MacIntyre and Dunne 2002, p. 9). On the other hand, it is conceptualized as 'relational practice' in the critique of the means-ends formulation (Noddings 2003, p. 242)[1]. In the teaching experience that I have had over the past few years, I have come to see teaching as involving building of mutual understanding and trust and thus a constant process of relating. While in my experience of teaching schoolchildren, this relational context has by and large defined my practice, at the university level 'in my case' this ethic has come to be largely mediated by the subject-matter[2]. For instance, most of the students who join the Master's programme in education (with which I am associated in the University) are women. Many also face socio-economic challenges that have a bearing on their English writing and speaking skills. The way, this intersection of gender, class and language shapes their aspirations, career choices and space to imagine alternatives, is a particular experience that unfolds in varied classroom conversations in the course, Curriculum Theory and Practice that I teach. Thinking through these conversations I constantly reflect on my positionality vis-à-vis the students and make attempts to contextualize the 'intentions' of learning that I talked about in the preceding pages of this write-up. More importantly, listening to these experiences enables me to critically reflect on the

1. I quote Noddings (2003, p. 242), 'When we look at the teaching-learning connection we have to agree that teaching is means-oriented. But, unlike medicine (which is also means-oriented), it often involves a relationship close to friendship and, in this aspect, it is not means-oriented. Moreover, learning is not the only end sought in teaching. At least, the learning of content specified in the school curriculum is not the sole end of teaching'.
2. Noddings (2003, p. 249) states, 'How might we describe the 'goods internal to that form of activity' called teaching…? First, schoolteachers accept some responsibility for the development of students as whole persons. The younger the student, the greater this responsibility. As the student grows older, the balance of responsibility shifts, but even the university teacher bears some of this responsibility… I still remember with great affection a university professor of mathematics who halted a lecture with a very stressed class to say, 'This isn't a matter of life and death, you know'. After a collective sigh of relief, we worked together to figure things out. We were encouraged to concentrate on learning and co-operation instead of competition and acing the test.'

subject-matter of the course and the programme of study. This has brought about nuanced changes in my research interests as well as encouraged me to engage with the intersectionality of gender, class and aspirations in education. I actively make attempts to integrate these explorations with the analysis that I bring to the classroom. At the same time, I also work towards a teaching-learning style (which itself in educational studies is the subject-matter) that encourages the students to make sense of these gendered and classed experiences as being shaped by a larger social phenomenon and to think around sustained responses (Apple 2013). Beyond the subject matter, I have found myself mostly not-so-well-equipped to offer 'help' to the students in 'solving' the problems they experience in their individual/personal spaces. Yet, it is also evident that different teachers have different ways of locating themselves on this continuum of relational practice.

The second, and related to the first aspect, concerns certain conscious efforts that one has to make to establish a working relationship with students—especially to enable them to reflect on and relate to the classroom discussions despite constraints. In the beginning of the course, I organize a discussion with the students on the norms of participation in the class. One major norm that I expect the students to follow is high attendance and contribution to the discussions. Students do not always follow these norms due to varied reasons. However, from the feedback that they turn in for the course it comes across that this encourages them to factor in their attendance and participation while assessing their own learning in the course.

I carefully note the expectations that students have from me and follow these to the best extent possible. These mostly overlap with the norms that my profession also establishes for me. I discuss the class and assessment plans with students. I return the graded assignments with sufficiently detailed and specific feedback within the timeframe decided. The assessment plan has provisions for revised submissions and I provide time to students for discussion on the feedback. All the class records are kept in order. At the same time, I have learnt to appreciate that each cohort of students brings its unique group dynamics to the classroom. The composition of each cohort is different and this has a bearing on learning. Thus, one has to think about the sequencing of the subject matter and assessment plans in the context of the unique positionality dynamics of a cohort.

Third, I have come to understand that teaching in a university programme is not an individual isolated activity. It assumes that teachers in a programme would dialogue on various aspects of their classroom experience. The presence and absence of this dialogue also shows in nuanced ways in the interactions with students and their overall experience in a programme. These programme teams are also microcosms of subject/discipline specific communities. Whenever I have had the opportunity to discuss academic aspects and teaching within my programme team, it has helped me in substantive ways. The meetings on the development of the MA Education programme and its courses during the first two years (2011-13) of the establishment of the School of Education Studies were particularly very helpful in inducting me in higher education as a faculty member. I have felt the absence of this dialogue on all occasions where it could not take place.

Along with the dialogue within the institution, my interactions with those in the field of policy and practice outside the university space have also influenced my approach to and preparedness for teaching. The work that I have done with the practitioners and institutions in the field, in varied capacities (of an observer, and a member of the national policy framing processes, a researcher and a member of a policy advocacy forum), has enabled in me a broader view of education—and of the complex relation between theory, practice and policy. This has brought a qualitative difference in the content that I transact in my classroom.

References

Apple, Michael W. (2009). On the tasks of the critical educational scholar/activist. In R. Winkle-Wagner, C.A. Hunter and D.H. Ortloff (Eds.), *Bridging the Gap Between Theory and Practice in Educational*

Research: Methods at the Margins (pp. 21-34). New York: Palgrave Macmillan US.

Apple, Michael W. (2013). *Teachers and Texts: A Political Economy of Class and Gender Relations in Education*. New York: Routledge.

Carr, D. (2003). *Making Sense of Education: An Introduction to the Philosophy and Theory of Education and Teaching*. London: Routledge Falmer.

MacIntyre, A. and Dunne, J. (2002). Alasdair MacIntyre on education: In dialogue with Joseph Dunne. *Journal of Philosophy of Education*, 36(1), 1-19.

Noddings, N. (2003). Is teaching a practice? *Journal of Philosophy of Education*, 37(2), 241-251.

Trigwell, K., Posser, M. and Taylor, P. (1994). Qualitative differences in approaches to teaching first year university science. *Higher Education*, 27(1), 75-84.

12

Reflections of a Teacher in Becoming

Shivani Nag

As I begin to organize and pen down my reflections on teaching, I am reminded of several incidents while undergoing my own formal education where an experience involving an interaction with a teacher was followed by a resolve 'to do things differently', if I someday found myself in the role of a teacher.

TThere were also those fewer but very significant moments where one felt inspired by a teacher. As I try to reflect on what made some teachers 'inspiring' while some only 'good teachers', I do realize that with the former, there was also a sense of being understood and received and not merely of 'receiving' and being enabled to understand. Since the experiences of being understood and received by a teacher formed significant turning points in my own journey of self, I thought it was a given that someday if I got into that role, I would attempt to do the same. Today, when I finally am in that role, I find myself revisiting those significant experiences. The revisiting is particularly necessitated because of the growing recognition of the different contexts from which the students come, contexts that are also often marked by sharp inequities. The revisiting is also necessitated by the acknowledgement of students as active agents who respond to and negotiate with their contexts and the university space. It is a learning that continues to be a work in progress and which also throws up several challenges and dilemmas as one proceeds.

In this write-up, one of the attempts will be to focus on these challenges and dilemmas that I continue to face in my pursuit to be an empathetic teacher who can facilitate educative experiences for her students.

As a teacher, when I try to empathetically connect with students, sometimes I wonder how useful is it to draw on my experience as a student whose own context was only one of the many that exists. But a little more thinking around the feeling of being understood that those few teachers were able to create is insightful. What they managed to create in a classroom was a culture of empathy, where to be a received was not a narcissist experience marked by the indulgent attention of a teacher. It was not an attempt to ease away a student's struggles or challenges or romanticize them, but rather allowing for space where a recognition of those became necessary and there was some sensitive space where their articulation could be enabled.

This insight becomes particularly significant in the light of some of the conversations that I have had with my own colleagues around empathy, where attempts to empathize seemed to be constrained by a limit around 'knowing the student'. 'How many of our students and how much of them can we truly know of to be able to empathize with all?' I struggled with this question when it was first put forth to me, and it is here that revisiting my experience of receiving empathy was helpful. Was the empathetic understanding I received as a student or continue to receive as a friend, a colleague and in the various networks of relationships I am embedded in, contingent to who knows how much about me? Is a tell-all narration of one's life struggles a pre-condition to receiving empathy? Does empathy follow 'knowing' or does it facilitate space where 'knowing' is possible? The revisiting has also enabled me to acknowledge my own failings where I did once put 'knowing' as a necessary condition for empathy and where I blamed my own lack of empathy towards a student on 'lack of information' that I felt maybe others could have provided me! And it is this interaction with a student that I want to write about. I want to write about it also because it was not until I thought about this incident in the context of a discourse on empathy that I was really able to confront some of my own contradictions vis-à-vis the process of empathy.

I was to supervise a dissertation of a student whom I had never taught. Perhaps too sure about my own ability to empathize, I told my students that they could share their struggles with me and it did not matter if they were struggling with language or writing in general, and that we could together work on the issues they brought up. I assumed that it was all that it took to inspire trust and create empathetic space. The particular student was extremely regular in terms of meeting me and in keeping-up with the various deadlines. I could see serious challenges in the use of English as a medium of expression and comprehension, but it took me months to realize there were some more difficult challenges around concepts. Having assured support and having assumed that my request to share struggles would on its own lead to them being shared also made me impatient. My focus on my own communication and positions made me unreceiving of the several non-verbal expressions of discomfort that were shared with me. Not only had I assumed that my asking was all that was needed for the others to share, but also I had assumed that sharing could only be achieved through verbal modes of communication. Each time I would ask the student if she had understood what I was trying to explain, I would get a nod indicating 'yes', and sometimes even a vocal 'yes'. When some days later I would receive a write-up that was conceptually no way near my expectation, I would react by asking why did she not tell me if she had not understood. I conveyed my requirements through verbal language and expected any understanding and non-understanding to be expressed through it. She expressed herself non-verbally and perhaps was far more receptive of my impatience, anxiety and urgency even if I did not voice them outright. With so much verbosity, clarity, determination and urgency exuding from my being, where indeed was the space to be unclear, unsure or confused. Could my 'being too sure' allow receiving of something that was 'unsure'? As the difficulty in communication increased and I became more aware of her challenges not through her sharing but through struggles she could no longer hide, I felt a sense of panic. There was too little time and there were many more challenges than I had anticipated. In this realization, I felt angry with colleagues who I thought should have voluntarily shared some of her struggles that they faced when they had taught her, assuming that it could have helped me understand her struggles earlier than I finally did. At this juncture, while I was able to reorient my efforts having somewhat understood her situation, my anger vis-à-vis my colleagues prevented me from reflecting on my omissions and inability to create space where she could have felt received and comfortable. I did gradually start being more mindful of my own anxieties and sense of urgency while working with her. We tried to meet outside the confined space of a cubicle, work at a slower pace and tried not to set too many targets and deadlines. We would begin by penning down some ideas in Hindi and then move on to translate them into English. In a meeting with colleagues, a suggestion also came up whereby we could formally request for additional time for her and the additional time helped immensely in getting her work ready for submission. Even after the submission and her viva where the presence of sensitive examiners saw her being able to speak about her work with a sense of ownership and confidence, I did think that the journey could have been better had I understood the struggles earlier. Importantly, I continued to evade any need for introspection since I held others responsible for my delayed understanding of her situation.

It was not till very recently when a discussion around empathy and my attempts to reconnect with my own experiences of receiving it, nudged me to revisit this encounter. As a student when I received empathy, it did not follow my sharing of a difficult experience. Rather, there were some teachers who through sensitivity in their 'being' created pedagogic space which I could enter, not having to leave my struggles outside. Also, entering with struggles did not necessitate their explication; however to not have to leave them outside ensured that they were not rendered invisible either. These struggles made occasional appearances in classroom discussions, through papers to be written, in one-to-one conversations and it was by way of becoming an active part of an engaged process that I who lived the struggles, also tried to understand them, negotiate with them and in the process, develop their articulation. What then made me in my role of teacher assume that my student would have already reached a thorough understanding of her struggles and have a ready articulation of the same? If I could not have understood my struggles in the absence of a context where they stood as challenges, what made me assume that my student could have acknowledged her struggles even before she entered a context that would see them become challenging? My articulation was facilitated through a process of active negotiation with them. How then was I unwilling to allow my student, the time and space needed to negotiate? What would have happened if I knew of her challenges beforehand? Would I have made tasks easier for her? Would I have conveyed to her that I understood she was having academic difficulties and in the process, provided her vocabulary to articulate difficulties that I was too impatient to allow her to experience and negotiate with?

As I come back to the broader concern around enabling empathetic classrooms, does empathy really require 'knowing' of all students, assuming they are 'beings' no longer in the process of 'becoming' or does it require the creating of a culture where patient, non-judgemental and non-infantilizing mutual receiving is encouraged? Can empathy be unidirectional in that it is only imagined as being given or received and not as giving and receiving? I ask this of myself as I now try to imagine how a seemingly confident, certain, determined and infallible teacher would have created space for mutuality where the student was reduced to receiving! How could I empathize with an anxious 'other' when I could hardly allow myself to acknowledge my own anxiety? How could I have created space for someone to be unsure, when I could barely be comfortable with my own unsureness about the other? Was it not knowing the other that obstructed my ability to be empathetic or was it not knowing the 'self' or at least not wanting to acknowledge certain parts of 'self' that formed the real obstruction? As newer questions begin to take shape which I do hope will find space in our collective deliberations, I realize that perhaps an empathetic classroom is also a space in 'becoming'...

13

Of Teachers and Students

Krishna Menon

Teachers and students—these distinct words evoke in me happiness and a sense of contentment and wholeness. I enjoy talking about my teachers, my students and the time spent in classrooms.

This reflection is about teachers and students, my teachers and my students, and my students who are now teachers. I would not be able to write about myself as a teacher without talking about my teachers from whom I learnt how to teach. I am not sure whether teaching can be taught, but it certainly can be learnt—by observation, like I did. I was fortunate to have some great teachers—Gurus. I am aware that the idea of Guru-Shishya Parampara understood conventionally is out of place in the secular and egalitarian context of the modern university. But who is a Guru? A Guru is someone who could 'transform the small one into a large one', in other words someone who can demonstrate the interconnectedness of learning and knowledge and thereby of life in all its forms. It is someone who can add gravitas (guru meaning heavy or large) to the experience and understanding of this world, but do this ever so lightly. I have been fortunate to have learnt from many such teachers.

I was exceptionally privileged to learn music from Vidwan Shri Shankara Sharma for nearly two decades. He learnt music staying with his Gurus, the famed Alathur Brothers.[1] He often

1. http://www.carnaticcorner.com/articles/alathoor_brothers.htm

told me about his difficult life at the Gurukula where manual labour and unquestioning obedience was the norm. He shared this without rancour and changed his approach to teach young students in the capital city of Delhi rather seamlessly. However, there was no compromise as far as the music he taught was concerned. He taught me the value of being disciplined, focussed, and committed in order to communicate and enjoy the exquisite beauty of a musical tradition. He sang and his students were expected to repeat after him. He would sing an aalaap and gently ask his students to place the scale and name the Raaga—there were no elaborate lectures on structures of Raaga and Swara, but through his singing he demonstrated the life of each Raaga to his students. He taught me the importance of presentation and the finishing touches while singing; he likened it to the bow on my schoolgirl ponytail! Such a simple analogy to convey a profound point about aesthetics and Rasa creation, that I cannot stop marvelling at his pedagogic insight.

Among the earliest teachers of Bharatanatyam who came to the Delhi was Guru K.J. Govindarajan, a highly trained vocalist, choreographer and nattuvanar.[2] I have learnt from him the interconnectedness of music, dance and poetry. As a young student, I watched him breathe life into a popular Malayalam film song by choreographing it within the grammar of Bharatanatyam. He was open minded and creative, secure in his knowledge of a great art form, he was quietly confident of applying his understanding to new and untested terrains. He showed me that categories of popular and classical are not rigid and the intent of the artist is of great significance. This was a great lesson for a young child to learn.

Guru Deba Prasad Das was the youngest of the Trinity of Odissi gurus, the others being Guru Pankaj Charan Das and Guru Kelucharan Mahapatra who are credited with rebuilding what we today refer to as the classical dance form, Odissi.[3] My teacher, Srinath Raut, was Deba Prasad Das' disciple and

2. http://www.thehindu.com/features/metroplus/society/gurus-grace/article6510748.ece

3. http://www.debadhara.co.in/guru-debaprasad.html

acutely aware of his lineage and responsibility. He taught me the importance of patience and encouragement. He witnessed my body's struggle, schooled in Bharatanatyam, to acquire the grammar of Odissi. He never described any movement or gesture of mine as 'wrong', but would helpfully suggest 'other' ways of doing the same thing. I learnt that the same idea could be rightly conveyed in many ways—each distinctive and valuable. Yet another important lesson learnt from my teacher, that I hope has found its way into the classrooms where I teach.

Very often, it is in and through pedagogy that a 'truth' is sought to be created. The Guru or teacher stands at a difficult crossroads—how to create a *Parampara* (tradition or corpus of learning) and yet demonstrate to the shishya or learner the tenuous, porous, and dynamic nature of the tradition? This is the question that grips every perceptive teacher. While *Parampara* certainly invokes a tradition, it is for the teacher to convey the powerful and somewhat iconoclastic idea that this discipline or tradition itself is constructed at a particular moment and should be examined from different vantage points.

I learnt this from many of my teachers and friends and students. Sudipta Kaviraj demonstrated that Marxism understood as a closed, formulaic and unilinear account of history would diminish the genius and creativity of the philosopher who famously asked for change. From my dear friend and colleague Nivedita Menon, I learnt how to engage with larger processes of change and draw students out of the confines of the classroom to the streets of the city and then back to the classroom in order to make sense of what was going on in the streets. From Neera Chandoke, I learnt the centrality of communication, that whatever is said in class has to be clear and yet elegantly stated—when combined with her formidable scholarship, it became an unforgettable experience. From Meenakshi Gopinath I learnt the importance of uncompromising academic rigour, professionalism, and warmth as qualities that are important for a teacher.

As a teacher, I have been fortunate to be able to interact with some of the most dynamic, intelligent and diligent young women of our country. Year after year, I have been impressed by their desire to break free and learn. Despite the rather rigid framework of the system that I was a part of, the young women who were in my class seemed aware of the precious opportunity that they had. I could not resist being drawn into their journeys. Each young woman had a story that was uniquely her own and her own struggles; however there was also something strangely universal about young women wanting to step across the thresholds that society fixed for them. I have had princesses from neighbouring countries, daughters of a dictator who was overthrown while still they were students in my class, young women from families steeped in feudal hierarchies, students whose families were involved in radical politics, and students who were the first in their village to reach university—all of them taught me that the courage to question and a deep resolve to change are what make education meaningful. To do all this with wit, charm and a certain amount of *sangfroid* is what I have learnt from them. It is almost incidental in my recollections, that I taught Politics in Contemporary India or Debates in Political Theory!

Many years have gone by and I continue to find this thrill of journeying with my students irresistible, now as a teacher of Gender Studies. Many of my students are now teachers, here in India and elsewhere—we exchange notes about our experiences and continue to learn from one and another. A tradition of teaching is surely there, of which I am a small part.

14

Instructor to Mentor

Teacher or Learner

Kuriakose Mamkoottam

As a child, I grew up dreaming to become like one of those I admired; and I did have people in my early life, I really admired. The top of the list includes some of my teachers at the junior school as well as those in senior classes during my childhood and adolescent years. I admired them because I saw in them personalities who shaped young minds and guided their thoughts. My early image of a teacher is someone who stood tall (not physically) with an imposing personality who could influence and impact other people, especially students not only in the classroom but much beyond in their lives. The teacher, to me, not only imparts knowledge to students, but also facilitates the bringing out of their inner talents and abilities to develop them into life skills. In addition, the teacher inspires students to inculcate values and instill aspirations that would earn them respect and recognition. I vividly remember some of the teachers in my early life; they not only loved me as a child and as a person, but also inspired me to nurture dreams and strive to attain my ambitions. For a very long time in my youth and beyond, I kept going back to them who continued encouraging me to remain steadfast in my journey of life.

After completing my undergraduate studies, I decided to take a break and teach in a school located in one of the district headquarters of North India. Along with teaching, I was also given the responsibility to assist a senior teacher who was in charge of the students' hostel. I spent a good amount of time working and travelling (during weekends) with him. His personality and behaviour drew my attention; I watched him closely and observed the way he dealt with students both within the classroom and outside. This US Marines veteran was admirable in his ability to enforce discipline in the students on the one hand and remain, at the same time, intimately close to them, especially by engaging in sports and games, which earned him their respect and love. In retrospect, I feel that my friendship and association with this senior teacher has made an indelible impact on me, as I myself became a (university) teacher later in my life.

After teaching in a school for a year, I decided to pursue higher (postgraduate) studies in Sociology, which brought me to the Delhi School of Economics, University of Delhi, where I came in contact with some of the best-known thinkers and teachers of Sociology and Economics. I consider myself fortunate that I could develop close relationship with many of the professors, some of whom, I still remain in regular touch. I consider this period the best phase of my life, when I began to realize that teaching profession has a huge impact within the classroom and beyond it extending to the future life and career of students. I realized how the quality of a classroom changed not only with the content that was provided by the teacher, but perhaps much more with the personality that the teacher brought with her/ him. This is when the belief in me that a teacher could influence the thoughts and impact the life of students far beyond the classroom developed into a conviction; and I had no doubt in my mind that I wanted to be a teacher and nothing else!

The classroom could be seen as a theatre, a sacred space, where live-drama is enacted out between the teacher and students, which is (expected to be) governed by a set of rules, norms and practices (both formal and informal). Everything that is largely driven by rules has a tendency to become rituals; and rituals usually create an attribute of 'sacredness', attached with sanctions and rewards. Like all other spaces of performance, classroom too often becomes a space, where teachers take their position on the centre stage and perform while students sit in the audience to watch/ view the performance; such performances may be enjoyed, disliked and criticized. It is also true that this dyadic relationship between the teacher and the student could be improved and improvised based on feedbacks and reflections. As a true performer, the teacher is expected to approach every occasion of the classroom interaction with a great deal of responsibility, with full preparation, keeping in mind what the students would be expecting from that interaction. While such classroom interaction may be seen as a mechanical transaction, it is also possible to see it as a deeply intellectual and emotional exchange of thoughts and ideas.

Now that I have spent over forty years as a member of the teaching profession, I can clearly see that my imagination of teaching, the teacher and that of the classroom has evolved and perhaps changed over a period of time since I started my career as a teacher. When I look back, I can clearly distinguish three different images/ roles, which I think a teacher would perform: *instructor, facilitator and mentor.* These different roles are perhaps simultaneous dimensions of the relationship, which if performed in synchrony, would enrich the experience of the teacher and that of the student, who are engaged with each other in the classroom and beyond. And yes, teacher-student association is perhaps one of the most fundamental relationships that has always been valued and cherished at all times. I often feel that a version of the teacher-student relationship is manifest in all forms of human interaction and engagement, a relationship that is based on the power of knowledge and information. The question of the implicit hierarchy in such a relationship, or any such dyadic process, is of course debatable. While there is an inherent hierarchy in all forms of exchange, including human relationship, which is also a form of exchange, this internal hierarchy itself could often jeopardize the very foundation of the relationship, much more than ensuring its sustainability.

In my early years as a teacher, I remember seeing myself largely as an *instructor*, who was given the onerous task of imparting knowledge and information to the students. I am sure all teachers who assume such a role would attempt to do their best to respond to the challenges that come along. As a young teacher, I would spend many hours preparing and rehearsing each word of the lecture that one would utter during the forthcoming classroom transaction. The enormity of the task came along with some amount of fear, apprehension and anxiety, especially the overwhelming anticipation about the delivery and if it would be received well or would face the peril of rejection. As an instructor, one would always want to make an immediate impression as well as influence the thoughts and ideas of students thus impacting their lives beyond the classroom. The transaction would be often driven by the content it carried which was largely knowledge-based and packed with as much information as possible, with the belief that students had limited or no access at all to it, except through the medium of the instructor. The satisfaction an instructor derives would rest almost always on the misplaced sense of power derived from the belief that he/she is the custodian of that knowledge and information. This relationship between the instructor and the student could often become a one-way process, evoking little response from the students, assuming that their silence could be taken as acceptance or appreciation of the instructor and what she/he would have delivered.

After a few years of my teaching career, I began to realize that teaching was not satisfying if it remained merely a one-way process of giving (knowledge/information) and receiving nothing in return. I began to see myself performing a role beyond that of an instructor; I thought I would become a *facilitator* enabling to develop a learning environment. I realized the futility of creating the facade or a protective wall around oneself and defending the infallibility of the teacher. What became equally important was that the classroom could be seen as a space for learning from the critical thoughts and inquisitive minds of the students. Teaching truly has to be good communication, which is complete only after receiving genuine feedback, not limited to applause and appreciation, from the students. And it became important to encourage a dialogue, discussion and critiquing during the classroom transactions, and the learning came from the shared space of the classroom, the dyadic interaction that took place between the teacher and the student. With this shift in the perception of the teacher-student relationship and that of the classroom, it is imperative that the pedagogy and the transactional style too undergo changes. The classroom becomes a space where the teacher-student interaction becomes a collective process, outcomes of which may be evolutionary, and may not always be easy to anticipate in terms of precise quantity and quality. This changed perception of the classroom space can also reduce the inherent hierarchy of teacher-student relationship and help to develop an open environment facilitating the process of learning, both for the teacher and the student.

As I advanced in my teaching years over a period of time, the realization came to me that the most enjoyable part of being a teacher is to be a *mentor* and if possible, to become a long-term co-traveller with the students in their journey of life. No doubt that as a teacher one would occasionally experience momentary highs and a sense of satisfaction from the interaction with the students especially during the enactment of the classroom drama. However, the lasting joy often comes from the relationship one is able to develop and sustain over a period of time, much beyond the classroom and its theatrics. Such a relationship is not likely to be a one-way process and would be free of any hierarchy. It is rather likely to be a mutually interdependent and respectful relationship. It may become very similar to the relationship that one develops within one's family, with one's own siblings and children, based on trust and respect. However, such a relationship can develop and survive only if a sound foundation has been established during the initial phase of the teacher-student relationship that begins invariably in the space of the classroom. A teacher would perhaps do well for himself/herself and the students if attempts are made to develop a non-hierarchical and mutually respectful relationship right at the beginning. This is possible if teaching is seen beyond the role of the instructor, but as a facilitator and a mentor. It is perhaps the mantle of mentorship that transforms the character of teaching and that of a teacher. With the passage of time and the onset of modern technology, the space of the classroom and the perception about teacher-student engagement have also undergone changes. It would be an enriching and rewarding experience if we could embrace the new methods and processes for engaging with the student in this changing scenario.

Section 4

A Teacher in the Making ... Always

A teacher can never truly teach unless he is still learning himself. A lamp can never light another lamp unless it continues to burn its own flame.

— Rabindranath Tagore

Photo credit: Dimple (Amreen) Oberoi Vahali

15

A Teacher in the Making ... Always

Anirban Sengupta

Unlike many of my present and earlier colleagues, I never had the dream of becoming a teacher! I accidentally joined a teaching position. While I never had any doubt about my interest in research, I was quite sure that I did not want to become a teacher! Over time however, what has made me stay back in academia is not research, but teaching. Once I got a taste of it I never wanted to leave it. The more I began to teach, the more I realized that teaching is not just about one's knowledge in or engagement with a particular field; it involves taking many difficult decisions in a labyrinthine space involving human beings. Given that teachers have to negotiate their way through a maze that is dynamic and ever evolving, today I realize that such a dilemma is an integral part of life of any reflective teacher's being. And it is this dilemma that integrates the personal and professional life of a teacher, if at all they can be conceptually separated. It is this awareness that has made me appreciate the philosophical value of what one senior colleague of mine told me during my early years as a teacher, 'We are never trained to be a teacher, we learn to become one while teaching'. Therefore, in this short write-up what I want to share is that the process of becoming a teacher is defined by the way a teacher identifies dilemmas in multiple spheres of his functioning and tries to take decisions around them. While I use the word decision, I do not attempt to claim that once decided, the dilemma disappears. Instead what I am trying to put forth is that decisions have to be taken as the 'practical' world in which we exist demands us to take decisions. In this world, there is little space for ambivalence. But dilemmas continue even after decision-making has been completed ... sometimes forever! I now will go on to write about some of those pressing dilemmas that continue to resound in my inner ear as I try to reflect on being a teacher.

1

While levels may vary, students of any class we teach are essentially diverse socio-culturally, psychologically, economically, politically, and therefore academically. This is more so in higher education as it is the end of the educational pipeline and all our students arrive to us in a half-baked form. There lies a limit to which we as teachers can contribute towards their transformation, even if we want to. One of the critical pedagogical challenges that surfaces in this connection is to find the level at which one should pitch the lecture or discussion in a classroom that is by definition non-homogeneous in terms of intellectual standards. In the past, there were occasions where I realized that at times I had to leave behind weaker students in trying to attain an academic level that I considered desirable. At other times, I felt I had lost the attention of the advanced students by trying to go down to the level at which the weakest student could be brought on board. Pedagogically, one is advised to pitch at the middle level while trying to pull up the weaker students and trying to provide more complex contents to the advanced students. Conceptually, this looks all right; in actuality, finding this middle level remains hugely challenging. It needs to be constantly rediscovered in every class.

An institutional solution to this challenge has been to offer tutorials preferably through teaching assistants so that faculty time is not spent on them. This appears quite convenient on the surface, as it not only spares teachers the additional workload, but also provides an opportunity to teaching assistants, who are often research students at the same institution, to earn some money and also gain experience. However, one of the practical challenges that arises here is the availability of space where tutorials can take place. This becomes quite critical in institutions (and they are not too little in number) that are battling with the availability of space for academic activities beyond scheduled lectures. A more serious challenge that one has to deal with involves deciding which students are expected to be part of this tutorial. Should they be only the weaker ones who need help or everyone? If a tutorial group is by definition meant for weaker students, the question that needs to be considered is, should weaker students be compelled to be part of this group or should they volunteer to join the same?

Engaging with the above questions is extremely critical as they design the way a tutorial group evolves and the social meanings that get attached to it. If a tutorial group is meant for weaker students, there exists a possibility that it would attract a pejorative label which its participants implicitly would have to bear. In this case, unless attendance is made compulsory, some of the weaker students who do not want to be so labelled may prefer to avoid this group. But then, compulsory attendance has its own problems; it presumes that presence by default enables learning and one can be compelled to learn by making it compulsory. Both these assumptions can be challenged pedagogically. The second challenge for a tutorial group meant only for weaker students is that the scope for peer learning from the more advanced students is missed out. On the contrary, if a tutorial group either involves everyone or if multiple tutorial groups are created that involve some advanced students and some weaker students, the challenge of the classroom situation reappears. One of my weaker students who has a limitation in speaking English and comprehending academic texts written in that language said to me in Hindi, 'I feel scared to speak in the class. Others in the class appear so knowledgeable and so confident' (translation mine). One must keep in mind that this is not true just for students who lack confidence in English. It is also true for students who can speak English fluently, but lack the capacity to engage with a topic in the way that academia considers 'desirable'. While on several occasions in the past, I made my practical decisions in this regard, I do not consider the issue to be resolved. The dilemma continues and I go on experiencing it anew with every batch of students I teach.

2

Evaluation has been an integral part of the process of education. The modern times are governed by a need for accumulation of symbolic tokens that can be carried across space and time. Accordingly, conferment of grades has become an essential requirement for education as a system. Finding a grade that exactly defines the performance of a student is a challenge for any reflective teacher and it ultimately is a subjective decision despite objectification of grading procedures by academic institutions. Here, a particular challenge confronts us with reference to weaker students. Based on my experience, I have always taken a position that weaker students are weak not because of their limitation in terms of intellectual capacity, but because of their personal biographies during their formative years, which after all is a matter of serendipity. Having taken this position, I consider it is unfair to evaluate the learning and achievements of all the students using the same parameters.

In evaluating the performance of weaker students, I have attempted to consider their past or present deprivation. I have also passed students when I felt that no immediate additional learning was going to take place even if the student was held back for one more year as many years would be necessary to make up for his or her deprivation. Such a philosophy of grading often violates the objective format of evaluation that most institutions of higher education develop for themselves. However, given the politics of meritocracy, it is not too difficult to understand why there is so much of stress on systems of differential evaluation. This poses its own problems. On the other hand, privileging weaker students does not by itself have any adverse effect on the more advanced students. What remains a difficult question to answer here is, does the practice of privileging and thereby letting 'underperforming' students leave the educational institution with their desired degree/diploma/certificate without developing necessary command over the knowledge and skills that the future demands from them end up doing justice or injustice to them?

The basis for this dilemma lies in the reality that at the end of the day, students need to find employment and a way to survive in life. For this it is desirable that they secure their future by seeking employment in areas where they succeed in acquiring some mastery, skills and knowledge during the years of their stay in educational institutions. This not only provides students a sense of security and satisfaction, but also makes educational programmes sustainable in the long run. Moreover, unlike academic programmes, usual workplaces are only concerned about finding a candidate who can do the work that needs to be done. Depending on how lucrative an employment is, even the best of students may experience fierce competition as candidates. Therefore, it is no surprise that workplaces have little time or interest in empathetically understanding a 'weak' candidate, his or her contextual background or in facilitating his or her journey ahead. Neither can the workplaces justify selection of weaker candidates leaving aside 'better performing' candidates, unless there is a legal provision for doing so. This may imply that weaker students, who graduated because teachers gave them the benefit of their earlier deprivation, do not end up securing the kinds of job they aspire for. Instead they may end up joining the mass of that frustrated category called 'educated unemployed' or the underemployed. Is this justice?

What if these students were held back till they completed acquiring the knowledge and skill to the satisfaction of educational institutions? That would surely mean that the students take more time to complete their education. In this context, one must remember that for many students, particularly for girls, coming out of home to study is still a special privilege that does not get extended if they do not complete their education within the scheduled period as marriage and not employment is written on their future card. For many others the actual cost of education (even where institutions do not charge tuition fees from students), and the opportunity cost of education (the other opportunities that a learner has to forego by being in a full time educational programme) are too much to be borne for any period beyond the scheduled period. For several, carrying it on for the scheduled period is also too expensive, both economically and socially. Therefore, in pursuit of quality, if educational institutions hold back the 'under-performers', these students may never graduate at all. They will instead join the list of 'dropouts'. Keeping this dimension in mind, I have often decided to do what has appeared as the most appropriate to me in a given situation. But my dilemma continues as to whether my action has been in service of justice or not.

3

The classroom is a social space and we teach human beings who have feelings and emotions, who go through different kinds of trauma, and who can even break down in facing specific situations of life. While some of these situations are temporary and disappear with time and with newer developments, others continue to remain and may even demand the intervention of experts. The classroom space, with syllabus to complete and with assessments to conduct, hardly gives any scope to understand what is going on in the minds of the bodies that we teach. Mental health in general, but particularly in a developing country like India, is a field that has not received the attention that it deserves.

It is not surprising to find teachers thinking that students make up stories about their psychological crisis as an excuse in front of an empathetic teacher to secure undue special privilege. And it is true that some students do actually take an empathetic teacher for a ride as it is very difficult to ascertain psychological distress through objective indices, which in themselves are very few. At times, teachers also argue that psychological problems like stress, anxiety, and panic that students undergo are largely self-created, by piling up pending tasks. Many accomplished young teachers who have been students in similar environments in which their students are presently studying, tend to further doubt and/or blame those students who hold work pressure as the reason for their psychological breakdown. The position from which these teachers argue is, 'When we were students just a few years ago, we never experienced any such psychological difficulty despite having similar or even higher work pressure. The students need to learn how to handle pressure and they can learn it only by being in pressure'.

There is some merit in this logic but what it does not consider is that all of us carry a subjective self that is distinctive in nature and all of us live our lives in contexts that are different from those of others. It may be true that some students dishonestly get or try to get extra time for themselves on the pretext of some psychological crisis or end up developing little capacity over the years to manage their work pressure. And yet how can one deny the reality of psychological difficulties that many of our students actually go through? Can we pretend that if we blame the students, they will always be able to 'rectify' themselves to attain 'normalcy'? I personally believe that it is better to encourage some dishonesty by being considerate, so that students who truly need such support are not left out. In spite of this, the issue poses a dilemma for me—in sensing the distress of a student, should we as teachers wait for the student to approach us or should we approach the student?

A large class is usually characterized by the distance that exists between the teacher and the students. Part of this distance is because of the imagination of the teacher-student relationship as being 'formal'. Part of it is also because of the perceived difference that exists between the identity of the teacher and that of students, including differences in their age and gender. Given that a sensitive issue like one's state of mind is extremely personal in nature, it is often felt that it can be shared only with those with whom one shares an 'informal relationship'. Rightly or otherwise, usually the teacher-student relationship does not fall in the category of an 'informal relationship'. As a result, it is usually friends (if any) who first get to know of an actual breakdown or an impending one in a student.

Even if teachers are not the first ones in whom students confide, several reflective and empathetically attuned teachers are observant of and in touch with changes in the behaviour of their students. And yet in a metropolitan culture, teachers, like many others, might choose not to ask students about their psychological states as these are considered to be private and therefore, not a topic of discussion unless the concerned person raises it. In times when individuality is on the rise, asking about someone's personal feelings without any initiation from the concerned person is liable to be perceived as a violation of personal space. The teacher who decides to do this often runs the risk of being labelled unnecessarily inquisitive and intrusive. On the other hand, in upholding the ethic of privacy one also runs the risk of not providing support to a person who may be in dire need of it. The reason why the decision to intervene or otherwise, poses itself as a heavy dilemma is also because an intention of doing 'good' through intervention must not end up in initiating an unnecessary sense of insecurity in the young mind of a concerned student that his or her psyche has all of a sudden become publicly visible to 'others'. The dilemma continues—how best can a teacher extend care to one's students, when is care called for and when must one's impulse to enter the psychological space of the other be held back?

The second dilemma in this context interestingly revolves around the creation of expert systems and expert identities in modern times. It involves further reflection on what one should do after one realizes that a person needs help. For physical illness, we know that one has to go to a doctor. This has been normalized by now and there is no stigma attached with such a practice. The same is however not true for concerns related to mental health. In a context like India,even a visit to a counselling centre can at times be stigmatized. Besides this there is a huge paucity of experts in the field. This waiting is often long and unaffordable for many. Moreover, there has been a large scale deskilling of lay persons, ever since we began creating expert systems for every field of life. This has given birth to a culture of referral to experts and expert systems for every problem we may face. In the process, we end up being relieved of our responsibility towards a fellow human being, as in the culture of modernity, everyone is and is expected to be 'busy' with whatever they might be involved with.

It is important to ask how far psychological difficulties are consequences of the fact that in our modern world, none of us has time for 'others'. While it is true that non-experts have limitation of capacity and specific individuals' lives demand expert intervention, the question remains, does everyone who is going through a psychological difficulty need an expert? This implies that we are required to reflect on how best can psychological problems be resolved through sensitive and empathetic conversations between fellow human beings as one makes oneself available to listen to and receive the life of the other. The more we abdicate our responsibility by simply referring states of human distress to experts, the more we lose touch with our ability to participate in a relational process. Also this may mean increasing the queue to reach psychological counsellors and psychiatrists for those individuals who are in desperate need for expert intervention. The question to face within oneself is that do we as teachers have the time or interest to talk to our students, when what they want to talk about has little or no connection with what we teach in classes or our research fields? And yet in spite of our efforts to be sensitive, the dilemma still remains—what if referral to an expert and not engagement in a conversation was what was most needed and desirable? How does a 'lay person' find a balance between the need to extend oneself to healing conversations and the tendency to quickly make a referral to an expert?

***

Let me end by saying that what I have tried to pen down in the foregoing account are a few of the dilemmas that I undergo as a teacher. While I take my decisions keeping the practical world in mind, dilemmas continue in ever-changing forms with every new experiential situation. At the end of the day, it is engagement with these dilemmas that helps me in reflecting on myself as a teacher. And it is through these reflections I realize my being as one who is constantly evolving as is the dynamic context of teaching and attendant challenges. Like when one is in a maze and the situation demands that one finds the way out, in going through dilemmas as a teacher, I take decisions because there are heavy consequences of ambivalence. And yet, like in a maze, ambivalence does not disappear with the decisions that might have been taken by me. Only engagement with ambivalence actually helps in continuously shaping and forming the teacher in me … forever.

16

Inside Classroom

Some Dilemmas

Vatsala Saxena

Conventionally, teaching is considered to be a linear transmission of knowledge, from a teacher to students. The traditional understanding automatically places the teacher on a higher pedestal—giving her a sense of authority and making her appear infallible. This idea makes me quite uncomfortable, maybe because authority does not come to me naturally. I am aware of the endless number of possibilities in teaching and I apprehend the danger in considering 'any' one of them as the 'only' one. I consider the classroom as not only a site of knowledge transmission, but also as a site of knowledge construction. Rather than seeking satisfaction in having complacent students nodding their heads to whatever I say, I feel accomplished if I can make my students think, question and express themselves freely. This often means that I do not have conclusive answers to my students' questions. It implies that we embark on an exploratory process together. Thus, the classroom becomes a place where the teacher and the students learn and evolve. However, working with this philosophy is not easy, especially with undergraduates who all their lives have been conditioned to follow rules and authority. Often, giving too much of space in decision-making to the students, opens up the peril of making oneself appear as an 'easy', or at worse an 'unsure' teacher. At other times there are situations where it becomes unavoidable to exercise authority—like in the context of examination and evaluation. I personally find the job of evaluation as a formidable ethical dilemma. At times, I feel that I am sitting on a seat of judgement and deciding a student's fate. I try my best to exercise academic rigour by maintaining as much objectivity as possible, and by providing justifications for my criteria of evaluation. Nevertheless it is not an easy task. It becomes all the more difficult, when students do not seem satisfied with the grading, and after discussing the rationale for the same with them, I may have to assume a disciplinary position and close the case.

There are days when I acknowledge in myself a certain kind of resistance towards taking a class. After some introspection, I have realized it could be a result of either one or both of the following reasons: (1) resistance to teaching arises whenever I feel I have nothing worthwhile/ new to offer to my students, and (2) when I feel inauthentic in the class. The above two issues are closely interrelated. In my attempt to take a good lecture, to make it interesting and to offer something new—I end up feeling like a performer, an entertainer, and thus feeling inauthentic. At times, while taking up a particular reading, I realize that it is plainly theoretical and boring yet important. However, my own narcissism urges me to say something profound and thought-provoking. In this paradox, either I tend to feel uninterested and demotivated in taking the class, or end up trying too hard to intellectualize things. I am also aware that the anxiety of doing a 'good' class takes away my spontaneity and mars the vitality of teaching as a lively process. If the lecture is too scripted and rehearsed, it makes me unavailable to the reception of newer ideas and imaginativeness that the students or the field of study could have brought up. I often try telling myself to be honest in my endeavours. I urge myself for a space to be non-perfect, for I consider authenticity, spontaneity and freedom to be valuable long-term goals of my teaching life. All of these come with their own struggles.

Just as teachers need to have space to be themselves, students too need space to express the way they want to. For instance, in the classroom, there might be students who are too verbose, who question endlessly and who often go off-track. Then there are students who are too dramatic. As a teacher I face the difficult task of not ending up discouraging such students and at the same time also trying to make the class more tolerant towards the 'deviant' voices. However, creating such possibilities is enormously challenging. The twin tasks require balancing between liberty and classroom integrity. I have to be mindful of ensuring that one (or a few) student's/students' liberty should not become the point of distress for others; or the situation must not end up becoming representative of the teacher's partial inclination towards a subset of the class or towards any particular student.

I feel uncomfortable in sharing that I feel it is important to mention how students can make a teacher feel quite vulnerable. I should also add that this might not be an intentional act by any student, but it acquires emotional meaning in that particular space, context and time. It could be as innocuous as not listening to a teacher, and thus making her/him feel unsure of herself/himself. Unfortunately, it could also be a possibility that a teacher feels insecure on account of her gender. Let me share my own experience here. When as a teacher, I enter a classroom, packed with students and struggle to get their attention, sometimes I tend to feel small, quite literally, 'one' against 'many'. As a young female, not a very well-built individual in a classroom full of students, many of them males, bigger and mightier than me, sitting quite comfortably on their seats, sharing a laugh, and turning a deaf ear to my repeated calls for maintaining silence and discipline, I do feel disempowered. I have this psychological realization, that I am a 'teacher' only because I am in the profession and by virtue of that they consider me to be their teacher, but otherwise I am a powerless nobody!

Lastly, I would like to mention the incidences of 'out-of classroom' interactions. When a student comes to me beyond the classroom boundary and shares some personal distress, often as a teacher of psychology I feel responsible towards him/her; but I may not really feel equipped to handle the student's distress or dilemmas all by myself. Also, the sharing by the student instils in me the dilemma that how much of the student's personal account should influence my classroom activities involving her/him? I try to extend empathy but sometimes I find myself unsure of how best to respond. These moments make me realize all the more that the role of a teacher comes with a lot of responsibility, not just for academic growth, but also for the entire 'self' development of her students. At the same time, I carry the awareness that it is courageous to be a teacher and more often than not, being a teacher means that one embarks on a journey of endless self-work.

17

Evocative Teaching

A Psychoanalytic Reflection

Ashis Roy

I have been teaching courses in psychology which are psychoanalytically informed. My teaching rests on a perspective that questions and reexamines the relationship between the normal and the pathological aspects of human behaviour. These courses are geared towards training the minds of students to prepare them to relate to states of psychological disturbance, which they would encounter and have to engage with in a variety of professional settings. Psychoanalytically informed teaching of clinical states orients students to look at human subjectivity as constitutive of many psychological parts, some of which are pain-laden and repressed.

Our society has little grasp of mental illness. By and large, it remains an unthinkable other. In my classes, I try to rework this experience of otherness by introducing phenomenological descriptions of states of mental illness to students which at times they begin to identify with. An uncomfortable but crucial exploration is introduced in classes through texts which question and reexamine the usual rift between intellect and experience. In the process, often the gap between the two is reduced and an emotional journey is initiated. Students start making sense of theorization by closely connecting it to their personal life. This journey into the self may carry a history of minor and major traumas. In this process many arenas of life such as intimacy, sexuality, awareness of one's body, depressed and 'dead parts' of self-experience, and one's subjecthood within the family unfold. For the teacher, this poses an ethical dilemma. A teacher may realize the long-term value of this form of teaching for fostering the professional development of students; however in the short run it becomes extremely challenging as students can begin to feel overwhelmed with the content and pedagogical processes deployed in classroom contexts. Here lies a pressing need for further enhancement of the professional and humane development of the teacher who dares to take his/her students through such an evocative pedagogy. In my case, I often struggle with ways of how best to hold and contain what has been unfolded in classes. In disciplines and subjects where subjectivity is explored and studied, I think the teacher too touches upon enormous vulnerability and does not remain the knower or expert. Certain kinds of fields do need special training for teachers as they involve themselves in modes of an immersive pedagogy.

Let me share a vignette from a class that has stayed with me. I was teaching the topic of psychosis. Psychosis is one of the most serious forms of mental disturbance and it is commonly known in society by the name of schizophrenia. As I was vocalizing the psychotic self through the writings of the psychoanalyst, Michael Eigen, I said that in a psychotic state, a person may feel that everything has turned into 'shit'. The psychotic individual fears that everything will get spoilt. These expressions were describing and evoking a quality of the deep anguish laced with mistrust which a person with psychosis may experience and for which s/he may not have words at his/her disposal. Non-psychotic individuals can also have psychotic parts in their selves. These could be characterized by chronic fears that nothing would work out and whatever they do it will ultimately be spoilt or destroyed. After the class was over, a student came and asked me, "Sir I have dreams in which there is a lot of shit. What does that mean?"

My communication in the class had evoked an internal image in her. The ideas and experience that I was communicating had given a form and shape to her self-experience which she in turn struggled to communicate to me. My invocation of experiential states had produced an identification and representation of something about her life that was shameful and unspeakable. The classroom was not the appropriate space to engage with her affective states in depth and an attuned clinical process would be required to explore various layers of the student's subjectivity. Such an awareness and subsequent knowledge of parts of oneself, through classroom evocations can induce in students the quality of being 'an other' to oneself. This troubled curiosity of the trainee can be held by the teacher who can help by encouraging the student to find a relationship with related texts, stories, films and an academic course. The fact is that many psychological experiences in the life of a student remain homeless and they look for space in the classroom and the university.

Another student studied obsessive compulsive disorder in women and looked at her own struggle with the illness. One of her major difficulties was also about seeing shit in her dreams in which gods and deities were smeared with shit. Amongst other things, shit can represent unacknowledged anger. Such unacknowledged inner aggressive forces can create immense psychological discomfort by impeding and interfering with the process whereby any person in one's relational world could become an internal soothing presence. Outer reality is thus experienced as threatening and destructive. Dreams and images of shit can also refer to intense shame that overwhelms and clouds self-experience.

The complex dimensions of human experience have often enriched our discussions about interdisciplinarity and the teaching of psychology in the School of Human Studies. Different perspectives of the subjective exist at the knowledge base of many courses in the psychology programme. At times, some students may experience mental blocks during assessments that demand an immersion on the part of the teacher to hold the student through trying phases. Different faculty members with diverse orientations are at the crossroads of discussing protocols and philosophies of assessment, the need to engage marginal voices in the classroom and to link texts to the life of the student. Grading has been given a subjective expanse in the grading scale adopted at Ambedkar University Delhi (AUD), where different scores fall on a continuum and this means that different students can coexist within a range of scores. Such a grading scale attempts to reduce hierarchies and competitiveness in the classroom. In the School of Human Studies, we have had several discussions on how the success of the student who is awarded the highest grade is linked with the failure of the student who performs poorly. One of the directions often discussed allows the preservation of the complexity of the subjective self. Upon being awarded an A grade, the successful student should be able to articulate the crises and the different steps needed to emerge out of the crises for the student who performs poorly. Such a student should have evolved and transformed different subjective states and crises into affective thoughts in his assessments. Crises evoke difficult emotions which need to be preserved with thoughts for the evolution of the subjective dimension in psychology. This pedagogical format reflects the sentiment imparted by the famous psychoanalyst Erik Erikson, who said, we only get to know ourselves in crises. Additionally, such a protocol aims at reducing the alienation that students who are situated at the extremes can experience by bringing them closer. The experience of being an achiever is definitely different from the one who performs poorly. If such a process is thoughtfully moulded with teaching practices, it gives us the opportunity for weaving the subjectivity of a student's life with the assessments

Teaching should be seen as an intersubjective process, in which the text is mediated via the teacher's subjectivity and consciousness. The classroom carries a charged atmosphere, in which the teacher can occupy many roles for the student and the student can occupy many roles for the teacher. Often the teacher is both an 'object'[1] of the student's phantasy and also

1. The term 'Object' in psychoanalytic thought refers to the internalized emotional resonances of significant relationships formed in childhood with our parents and other caring figures. These internal affective flows from our past have an unconscious internal presence which mediates the conscious experiences in our lives. As students we place these experiences onto teachers and as teachers we place these experiences onto students.

a real person with whom the student is forging a relationship. The assignments that the student writes are not only for one's intellectual advancement but also for the 'eyes' of the teacher. The teacher-student relationship carries a necessary idealization which helps the growth of both individuals. But this has to be bound by limits. Both teachers and students need to be aware of what they bring from their own lives which can colour and make them more sensitive to what they say and what they receive. As a psychotherapist in the university, my ongoing professional training constantly focuses on and examines the intense dyadic bond between patient and therapist which is in service of therapeutic healing. This bond however also carries a lot of responsibility. Likewise, I think as teachers, we need to be responsible about the subjective states we bring from our own pasts into the classroom because we are in the position of authority. Being in authority, does not translate into the feeling of being in authority. Our subjective states can unknowingly open a lot in the internal world of the student. Both teacher and student can be carrying homeless self-states within them which shape the vicissitudes of teaching and of the teacher-student relationship

To conclude, teaching needs to be an immersive and self-questioning experience which can explore and engage with psychological difficulties that students endure. Assessment and evaluation needs to be envisioned in a way that the subjective complexity is not lost and can become a part of strengthening the class as a unit.

Reference

Eigen, M. (2004), *The Psychotic Core*. London: Karnac.

18

Who Teaches? Who Learns?

Suchitra Balasubrahmanyan

I regard a teacher's role as one of accompanying students on a journey of self-discovery. It is a mutually osmotic encounter and in the process, the teacher also learns something about herself.

Design, more than other disciplines, in my opinion, offers great opportunities for self-discovery, offering at once the space to soak up the world through the senses, engage with people and landscapes, be moved by these encounters, and represent these by visually working with one's hands quite tangibly. Then there is the space to respond, guided by one's inner expressive impulses as well as one's analytical self, to somehow transform the world around us into a better place. There is an aesthetic pleasure that awaits at the end, which can also turn bittersweet.

Design is also a discipline where students' inner world appears quite directly, even literally, in their work, inviting a teacher to engage both with the course and assignments at hand and the inner being which is engaging with those tasks. This is not an easy invitation, for both the teacher and the student, mostly because of the unpredictable ways that it happens, when the most (seemingly) innocuous task precipitates a challenge.

Let me give some examples. In the *History of Design* course I teach, I ask students to bring family albums, going back to their grandfathers' time if possible. Students enjoy looking at images of their own family and of others, and with deep engagement, stories come tumbling out. A lot of rich visual material from different parts of India comes into the classroom along with intergenerational narratives, social contours, celebrations, rites of passage, and memories providing evidence to piece together subcontinental histories of objects, the home, fashion, work, travel and lifestyles.

I can say a lot about this assignment and its deeply satisfying outcomes for a student. For one, the assignment was an unexpected turning point, anchoring her deeply in the material culture of her community and informing her professional work ever after, bringing her international acclaim. The same assignment could precipitate a crisis as it did for a vivacious, intelligent young woman, eminently capable in other assignments, who got a poor just-passing grade on this one. And I learnt the reason seventeen years later when I met her again and all she could speak of was the poor grade I gave her all those years ago. Her parents had at that time separated, she stayed with her mother, and the family photo albums were with a father who was no longer in contact. The assignment could not be done; even looking at other students' family albums was unbearable.

The drawing class is another setting where the self is revealed. The lines on the paper—sometimes sure, sometimes tentative, indecisive, sometimes careless, overconfident—provide a glimpse of the inner individual. It is a deeply satisfying experience to work with students, helping them to reflect on their work, see them gathering courage and confidence and share their surprised delight in the way their images gain strength and character.

Occasionally, drawing precipitates a crisis such as the discovery of finding a twenty-year-old student drawing like a three-year-old. Chairs, tables, plants—each drawing task was completed in a few restless minutes and each image was a clear representation of another being inside, at a stage different from his chronological age. I was plunged into confusion, drawn into the student's visual world while being taken aback by it, and had no experience in handling the situation from the pedagogical point of view. I had no resources to engage with an adult-child, and it also conflicted with my use of such categories as 'adult' and 'child' to make sense of the situation before me. No one could help me with this, neither colleagues in my own discipline nor others. I went ahead by instinct, blundering on with an assignment of drawing one's reflection in the mirror. Inexplicably, the pace of working slowed, and the images resembled the student, the details of body and clothes became recognizable. But I was unable to sustain this breakthrough for the student who returned to the earlier mode of working. I was told later I could have 'harmed' this student psychologically. I was terrified I might have destroyed someone in thinking of drawing as a reflective process which could be helpful in some way.

So what I am saying is that as long as classes and courses proceed predictably, the teacher feels satisfied, rewarded and affirmed that she has been able to successfully accompany the student through self-discovery. But when situations sometimes turn fragile without warning, the teaching-learning process feels unexpectedly dangerous. At such moments, roles get reversed and the teacher needs to become a learner. In such a situation, it might be that the teacher needs first-aid as much as a student. Perhaps more…

Or perhaps, if we think of such encounters as mutually osmotic relationships, there is nothing really like 'teaching'; only learning for both students and 'teachers'.

Section 5
Metamorphosing from a Caterpillar into a Butterfly

He who knows paternal strength
But still retains maternal greatness
Becomes a universal channel of everlasting grace.

— Lao Tsze

Photo credit: Shyam B. Menon

19

Fugue to First

Some Movements in the Melody of Empathy

Ashok Nagpal

Introduction

The following essay is in the form of an ongoing commentary, reflecting on the conscious and unconscious flows in a Psychosocial Clinical Studies class in progress at AUD. The writing is designed to take the reader right into the throbbing heart of the classroom where many things begin to unfold. Uncertainty and chaos get in-gathered into moments of surprise, discovery, joy and meaning and ultimately a more comfortable preservation of as yet unknown.

On 4th April 2018, the students of M.A Psychology (2nd Semester), played a prank on me. Eager to remain true to the psychoanalytic spirit of receiving all experiences non-judgmentally, I met the students' jest with enthusiasm and spontaneity. I felt like engaging because of a certain flow in me as I was reaching the class. I am glad, both students and myself, eventually managed to direct the classroom processes into a deeper exploration of several compelling concerns of value to young lives. This we could accomplish by burrowing into 'The First Psychoanalyst' an essay by the renowned psychoanalyst, Erik Erikson. Presented on the centenary celebrations of the birth of Sigmund Freud, the essay by Erikson, oft-cited in psychoanalytic literature, revolves around the three foundational principles through which Sigmund Freud interwove clinical practice based phenomena with theoretical formulations into a new discipline and a new profession. (Some of the relevant passages from this text are indicated in the following writing). The 'First' in the title of this essay also illustrates Freud's (the first psychoanalyst's) struggle to discover aspects of the discipline which focus on the unconscious, sexuality, ambivalences, wishes, fears, desires, conflicts, dreams and so much more in our psychic life.

My narrative intends to preserve the quality of the actual happenings as they took place in a two-hours long class. Through this sharing, I hope to delineate a form of teaching which is based on processing experiences, even as part of thinking keeps contact with the established tradition of thought, i.e., psychoanalysis.

April 4, in year 2018 was an unusual day. Erik Erikson's essay, The First Psychoanalyst (Erikson, 1964) (an essay which I have lost count of how many times I read in the last thirty years of teaching psychoanalysis) had come to grip me this year in an unprecedented way. For the first time, I came to note a special meaning in the opening sentence.

> It is a solemn and yet always a deeply incongruous occasion when we select an anniversary to honor a man who in lonely years struggled through a unique experience and won a new kind of knowledge for mankind. To some of us the field created by Sigmund Freud has become an absorbing profession, to some an inescapable challenge, to all the promise (or threat) of an altered image of man. But any sense of propriety, pride in the man to be honored this year should be sobered by the thought that we have no right to assume that we would have met his challenge with more courage than his contemporaries did in the days when his insights were new. It seems fitting to use his centenary to review some of the dimensions of lonely discovery. (ibid, p. 19)

I wondered to myself about the kind of incongruity Erikson referred here; how it had escaped me thoroughly in the last so many attempts, as I had been swung by the masterful concision that Erikson created in those three principles (cited later)—at once preserving the complexity yet speaking to each one of us as teachers and readers. What had made me remain so excitably fused with the path-breaking directions in the "Principles" as to miss out on the 'threat of an altered image of man'; what made me not register the enormously lonely aspect of Freud's work, what tumult had covered my oversights—I was still tumultuous in my reminiscences!

Walking down for my class with the Second semester students of MA Psychology (Psychosocial Clinical Studies) for a course called "Reading Freud", I was particularly close to the question about how to facilitate this process in ushering in a new faith in the First of the identity of a new profession—a profession which possesses a blend (with its unique conception of clinical phenomena) of a special avowal of the personal-subjective process as well as a technique of engaging (and intervention) with mental illness in all its myriad variations. And my preoccupations were involuntarily drawn to my memories of schooldays. Having been a student of biological sciences till my graduation years before I had stepped in to take up psychology, I found a navel of sorts in Erikson's demonstration of Freud's "laboratory" where he had discovered his new approach!

Memories of my schooldays got copiously stirred. They included the not-so-clean chemistry laboratory, pungent hangovers from repellent hydrogen sulphide and striking though eerie colours, lent to flames by various liquids and gases during the experiments; the gleaming apparatus in the physics laboratory, so one could be seduced into pristine participation with air, light and water, as also the unforgettable odd memory of a dead salamander in preservative fluids in an air-tight jar in the zoology laboratory which somehow never failed to leap at me from behind, as it happened this time too! Had I not been in the grip of a dream-like state, yet to fully dawn in my thumping head whilst my springy hands clutched a book as I moved towards the classroom N3 to join the class on Reading

Freud? What is the laboratory that I have missed having reached the age of sixty-five? Have I just come upon it though its doors are not fully open yet? Why do I need students to reach this heightened state of community for the future of my discipline? Is the old, a perennially old crisis slowly yielding? Am I managing to gain a measure of it in some dimension? How to reach what Erikson brought up—Schooling in Method? Where is the laboratory for a psychologist like me, trained in Experimental Psychology and gaining my depths ever so slowly whilst barely managing to keep myself together vis-a-vis my own flows in psychoanalysis? Why does this sheen in my memories of science laboratories not manage sufficiently to hoodwink this torment when it comes to my love, my most cherished discipline, psychoanalysis!! But this time, I have carried it for nine weeks. I have reached a fanatic intensity, an expectant enunciation; I can break through the mystery of the First. I am sensing-registering, through brilliantly set-up rhythms of processes and paradoxes in this essay that FIRST Freud is not to be just known as a birth having happened in the past! I was in earnest touch with the artist in Erikson, who has given us an amphitheatrical set-up as well as a configurational passage so that FIRST can be conceived anywhere at some point. And I am gathering its shape well by slowly reading in the class, line by line and paraphrasing these twenty-eight pages of the essay in this course on Reading Freud. It has a rhythm to its reverse swings, special sorties to land in depths aesthetically and discover the ethics in the amniotic fluids. Not many would inaugurate a celebratory talk given on the occasion of 100th birth anniversary of Sigmund Freud with a powerful irony such as I noticed so late, so late in my reading only this year.

I have reached the corridor of N3. I will soon see that alive presence of activities amongst students, eating gracefully, and gossiping spicily, a few of them in a cluster appearing somewhat worried and yet with no particular indications of waiting such as I associated with the teaching in my heydays.

But no, what I see today is unusual!

There are lights near the anterior part of the room focusing on a woman-student sitting in a chair as close to the teacher's chair as half a meter, in the very face of the teacher if he does not pull his chair apart! All other students have meticulously pulled themselves close to the walls of the classroom and very few lights have been kept on. A stage has been set, heightened further by a play-act demureness on this girl's face whose name I have not come to know in all these weeks. The young woman is clearly holding on to this unusual setting and, like me, is visibly nervous. Do both of us stand a chance of working in this clime?

'Schooling in Method?' That phrase by Erikson saves me from being overtaken either by a stunned state or defensive jocularity aimed at unravelling the mystery of this arrangement. What a coincidence! A "laboratory" has been set-up! Replicating the way an Experimental psychologist works with his subjects conducting experiments, with a screen in between occasionally. The seating arrangement duplicates that. Where is the conventional screen then? I cannot see it clearly in the dimly lighted room; it is knocking at me in the impish avoidant looks on many students' faces. As I reach closer to my own chair to assume my seat, the sheepish downcast look with smiles at the corners of Surbhi's mouth (the girl seated right in my face), the screen forms itself.

I pick up a playful tone, demanding that my confederates remain scrupulously vigilant whilst closely monitoring my performance today. I wonder loudly what grade would I obtain, given this closely located teaching inspector of the yore, sent to assess me!! The class laughs. Now I can pick a tempo to ask them more about how this seating arrangement came about.

Surbhi explains how she was absorbed in some activity so deeply that her classmates sensed an opportunity and played a trick on her. Matching her self-absorption with their noiseless sliding away, the entire group moved closer towards the three walls. Before she/anyone could realize, an undeliberated 'first' has been created in the centre. And something is stuttering around this creation, an afterthought of some kind. Surbhi continues to wait to assess whether I would sense more and inquire after it. What more—I ask, by now made bolder by the game that had been set-up through a young collective unconscious mechanism. With a stammer in her speech and nervousness in her gestures, she reveals ever so slowly, a wager that was subsequently made amongst the students and herself.

If she can face Prof Nagpal so squarely for an entire span of nearly two hours sitting like this—there would be a treat!!

'Is it really Surbhi? Is it just a treat?' Hahaha in the background! Surbhi turned in a meekly soft yet clear response. No not just treat but money is at stake; whoever wins, an unspecified amount of money will also be won by that side!!

So there is a simulated battle between the Teacher and the Taught, enacted through close interfacial angles and matching of wits such as emerge when we are so absorbed as to be beyond interruption. Had the prankster reached a quick flash, having seen Surbhi in that self-absorbed state of intense retreat, that she is the best fit to combat a teacher who too every now and then gets lost to them during classes through his own reveries!! Aren't they constituted of the same metal? I am wondering what this close vigil/closeness is amplifying beyond being accustomed to having done Psychology Experiments in undergraduate years till just two years back! Has the student taken upon herself to suggest the requirement of a rapport that is lacking before more complex symbolic work by the Teacher could get foregrounded? I am quite unsure what is being raked up in the labyrinth.

I get drawn to see another unusual feature of the play-in-laboratory-scenario in this room; to our right is seated a student with prefectory intent as it were, lest the zones of such heightened duel slip out of control. On her right index finger, is tied a white helium balloon nearly merging with the white ceiling, a tower point to install an invisible but ever-present apex of thinking in the class announcing a striving for peace amidst unmentionable strife— is it? Or is it all my imagination? I have a need to settle so the class could begin but I possess limited knowledge about this mighty obstacle. The all-knowing older mode of tradition and teaching is getting tested by celebratory modes of wager, food, balloon, and money as forces that are preeminent in this youthful assemblage. The student group is suggesting wordlessly: remember we are located here to gain grand knowledge that you intend to bring through a luminary—Freud in the history of ideas in psychology—the Father of psychoanalysis. We are in your face lest you forget!

Erikson's formulation of three psychoanalytic principles, operating in the Clinic, begins thus:

> One can study the human mind only by engaging the fully motivated partnership of the observed individual, and by entering into a sincere contract with him. (ibid, p.29)

I must wrestle with these aspects even though this is not a clinic in a strict conventional sense. Yet students were curious, too curious in that moment to let any part slump into an active overwhelming state akin to patienthood. Lurking beneath this demeanour, is located an impulse that dramatized an active face-to-face encounter without a screen while retaining a playful (maybe partial) trust reposed in me, not to forget the somatic (or is it psychosomatic?[1]) need that the student Surbhi has negotiated within herself to assert as a dare: namely to bring firmly a mind-in-student closely seated to the dynamic flow that we expect from a Teacher's Being as well as through a shy display, propped up by peer presence, to contain complex moments.

I recall a marked ambivalence in Surbhi about acknowledging of what does one "win" in this contest? Surbhi had not wanted to bring in any mention of money! She was content to leave it at a 'Treat'. A direct reference to one's investment in money in setting up negotiations such as this one—I could also recall, had produced in me an urge with a different mix than I could immediately get a grip on. The impish chorus of others overcame the hesitation and helped me to connect with the

---

1. Surbhi had later shared, she had changed her usual seating position from side rows to a central one to avoid developing a headache that she gets from long periods of sideward looking.

larger troubled zone that is ever around as a shadow. When we establish private practice and charge money for our work of assisting in healing others, we betray our obligations to a staunch tradition of spirituality in our society. Investments of time and effort thus get overjudged and impede the establishment of our practice as a profession. Fortunately, the processes in metropolitan towns are changing rapidly. No wonder, Surbhi thought 'why not earn money on winning the bet? Why just a non-computed treat?' As she said afterwards "I experience no personal hesitation in taking money for work done for others". She seemed to have overcome her need to protect me/ herself/ both from the initial embarrassment.

Erikson's formulation of the second principle in Freud began resonating in my mind:

> You will not see in another what you have not learned to recognize in yourself. The mental healer must divide himself as well as the patient into an observer and observed. (ibid, p. 29)

I decided to stir some curiosity in them through offering examples of practitioners in psychoanalysis going on with their practice as late as in the eighties. In a couple of outstanding cases, books were being written by two women psychoanalysts after they become grandmothers. And what is more inspiring is that the works thus compiled, benefited from this stage-specific preoccupation whilst advancing the concerns and contributions of the earliest life-stages. Could we consider ourselves as especially fortunate to possess exclusiveness in the profession that gets predicated on a life stage theory—from birth till death, thus attempting to continue with a saga through clinical engagement ?—I ask the class. The very thinker, Erikson, whose essay I am sharing with you, I go on adding, has proposed this theory of nine life stages where the central tasks of each stage are conceived not just in directions that are idealistic; rather at the centre of his conception of life-stages, is the notion of crisis, as uniquely defined as a potential turning point, not just in the subjective life of an individual(s) but also in their community.

Indeed, this continuum of the developments, coursing through necessary crises, and demonstrating an intertwined presence in individual lives as well as institutional dynamics is one of the special contributions of Erikson's work.

A student Madeeha poses a question, bringing up a graver aspect that I must confess I had not come upon myself ever.

'Working for such a long part of one's life is quite alright Sir but how about dying on a patient/analysand? Don't you think it has traumatic consequences for the patients who are left behind?'

In my over-passionate identification, I had clearly neglected this aspect. Madeeha has possibly by now caught on my internal daze and picks up the courage to extend her sharing in the class. She continues to say,

'it has happened so often in my life that no relationship has ever said Bye to me before leaving'.

I feel a certain heaviness; the class may have been brought to a brink where sadness and grief shuts out so much. Am I conscious of the close look by Surbhi into my inner happenings even as I attempt to restitute this seething interruption by joining Yudhishtira, a character in the Hindu epic Mahabharata, who wondered aloud about the greatest riddle: how is that no mortal being thinks about his/her own impending death and goes about life as though he is not going to die ever? I think of Erikson's far more detailed case study 'The Nature of Clinical Evidence' which centers upon one of the briefest dreams in the history of psychoanalysis. There, too, a surgery in the life of an ageing analyst (Erikson) had triggered a deeply-embedded trauma.

One must not promise a child such certainty, and then leave him' (ibid, p. 67)

And a little later Erikson writes:

> ... the analyst had to go through the experience of a certain indignation that he was required to do an impossible work, namely, (the patient) had challenged me to prove all at once

> the goodness of mothers, the immortality of grandfathers, my own perfection, and God's grace. (ibid, p. 72)

I was struggling with how to transport the class through this grief; I doubt if I managed to betray it to anyone except maybe Surbhi. Like the patient mentioned in the above paragraph, Surbhi was too close to miss out my discomfort here. Erikson's formulation of the third principle could assume a meaning

> Psychological discovery is accompanied by some irrational involvement of the observer, and that it cannot be communicated to another without a certain irrational involvement of both. (ibid, p. 36)

The irrational was in ascendance. If analysts continue to practice till so much later in life, they are required to negotiate a charge of being heartless towards dying on their patients. Or even worse that they were practicing a pursuit of private-personal needs at that late, a stage, which the younger patients can legitimately protest: 'Why should even the therapist burden them yet again? Has not life already done this to them so much?' My own mild protest to bring in the only lasting truth of our dying, remains confined to my silence. Tenderness towards Madeeha as well as others in the class overtakes in this moment. Death as ever present in living can wait even as it needs no invitation!

Douglas, a student, helped by raising his hand and requesting a break of a few minutes. I heard him refer to his being thirsty. I was inclined to let go of the moment particularly as I was wobbling and looking for passages to bring in what was a distant subject for communication: how to look at internalizations in analytic work stamped with a thoroughgoing candour on the part of both the analyst and analysand (patient who also possesses a potential aspiration to become an analyst) in such a circumstance of the death of a working analyst of an age where death can happen naturally and is not premature? It is highly probable that this would appear in the free associative processes in sessions. However

Madeeha's grief is not shaped by any current loss but in terms of the old goodbyes not having happened!1 Indeed I was beginning to sense that I too became "thirsty" to drink it up more fully: a psychoanalyst derives his direction of long committed work, one might add, with an aliveness, to represent a purposefulness which is not too awed by impending death. There is the need to achieve this through becoming less feisty and more sober pattern that facilitates internalizations and in turn de-dissociates the gaps. Is it not possible to entertain an intensification in the analysands who have lost analysts whilst their personal work is still incomplete? Is it not likely that such an individual is left, after necessary living through the shock and grief, to reach a more determined bid to complete the internal form more concertedly with whatever means and resources that could still be marshalled?

These were some of the internal pointers that made me ask Douglas to postpone the need for a break for a while, sit next to me and help me read just one more paragraph so I complete the immersive communication somewhat better. He is a trekker and a great sport who did not disappoint me. Indeed he told me he needed to splash water on his face to wake up more fully! I think he read one of the following two passages:

Once Darwin embarked on the Beagle, however, and on his way to his 'laboratory,' he showed that dogged that prejudiced persistence which hone the condition for an original mind's becoming a creative one. He now fully developed his superior gift, namely, 'noticing things which easily escape attention, and observing them carefully. His mind proved ready for the laboratory and the laboratory seemed to have waited for him. He could employ sweeping configurations of thought which had ripened in him: cutting across existing classifications which assumed a parallel, linear origin of all species from a common pool of creation, he saw everywhere transitions, transmutations, variations, signs of a dynamic struggle for adaptation. (ibid, p. 21)

And another passage that Douglas read:

As we now turn to Freud, the psychological explorer, I hope

> to make the reader wonder whether anybody, but one, at least temporarily afflicted with psychosomatic symptoms, one temporarily sick of his own kind, could or would investigate his own species—provided that he had the inclination, the courage, and the mental means of facing his own neurosis with creative persistence. A man, I will submit, could begin to study man's inner world only by appointing his own neurosis that angel with whom he must wrestle and whom he must not let go until his blessing, too, has been given. (ibid, p. 23)

Douglas in delving into this reading underwent a salutary change. To my surprise, he now expressed his reluctance to take the break. He had woken up into a more energetic self; as if the thirst and/or sleepiness also expressed his personal struggle to go away from the akhara—tired as he and many others had become, with listening and listening to others, a passivity that needed to trek outward. I guess with all his trekking credentials, he could gain a better inspiration with the imagery of wrestling with an angel hidden in one's neurosis.

A break of ten minutes was taken nonetheless. Madeeha walks up to me during this break since I have not left the class. There are quite a few others who are also present. Madeeha adds a few more personal details about events of abrupt loss through death. It will help the reader to add here that she is a resident of Kashmir . I notice a sense of freedom that she has gained in her communications with me even as I appreciate her about her perceptive question.

Soon after the break as we reassembled in the class, I opened the address by sharing my own excitement more fully of having been made a part of this spontaneous experiment ! Surbhi commented how she does not feel embarrassed about taking money especially when one of the students had walked up to her to give her a ten-rupee coin as a mark of applauding her sheer guts for not having quit the hot-seat! It also indicated that she was winning the bet all the way. Usman raised his hand to ask a question, in the middle of my talking. By the time I finished my thought and turned to him to take over and acquaint us with his concern, he seemed to have forgotten it.

This happened twice at different points of time. And the class seemed to have taken it in their stride with laughter that was increasingly putting us at ease.

Two difficult questions were now posed by two students, Shreya and Prakriti, who had been registering their emotions in the class in a level-headed way.

First, Shreya: 'If you say Dreams are a representation of the truest democracy and utmost of freedom in the human psyche, how does the law of Psychic determinism as posited by Freud hold sway?'

I know in being drawn in by this question, we are knocking at the royal doorway into psychoanalysis, the combat and correlation between manifest and latent contents, between symptom and sublimation, between flight and roots, and no less, in the context of this essay, the twinning of art and science perspectives . One's own understanding at any point of time shifts, as it were, one is standing in quicksand. You may be fortunate and discover eggs buried in the sand that are ready to release the hatching newer beings. Dreams with their newer meanings too show that at their very root, is a "cause" which is determined by a primitive process/ capacity; that a baby state has been cherished and played with, in ways that are unspecifiable. Yet to the discerning eyes, such as Darwin's and Freud's in this essay , a set of forces, and patterns that lead us towards foundations is never easy to give up. A melody inaudible to the outside but constantly humming in the minds of the genius, who thus witness infinite forms all devolving at this fount. Afterall, forms in all their diversity are derived from a few basic patterns just as language in its inexhaustible forms of expression comes out of a few specific number of alphabets or music in all its unplumbable depths, comes out of seven basic swaras (sounds). Psychic determinism in contemporary psychoanalysis is rarely spoken about. That does not mean it has ceased to exist. Just that we do not stop to take an assessment of it, crises that affect us and slow us down make us aware of forces that are determining our march and only by locating newer mechanisms appropriate to the particular life-stages (psycho-sensorial axis as suggested by Bolognini, 2008) as well as socio-political context, do we regain the motility thereby generating that freedom designed from within. This is closest to the democracy of dreams, playing and mutuality of relationships.

I do not recall what I stated to the class but I trust my readers can appreciate that the spirit of this address demands we feel closer to the baby, the child, and engage with the home surround, the mother in order to discover the father in her (mother's) imagination, as being transmitted somewhat harmoniously to the baby. In so thinking, we may overcome threats that loom over fugue states and witness children imitating objects and others to discover themselves and ecstatically, creating "firsts."

Shreya seemed more than satisfied to me in the class. Yet in her writing which I invited from all those who had actively participated in this class, she also gifted me with this term Fugue, (especially as having been first used as a device in musical compositions to be interweave imitations and repetitions and contrapuntally developed to register opposing affects) suggesting it not be seen as anything but the laughter present in a skull as many of us can apperceive it!! The image is attached below. I am also grateful to her for various consultations that I had with her, in a bid to give body to what was a skeletal piece initially before it itself has grown into a FIRST—now.

The second question by Prakriti was to address the gender-bias in the theorization of psychoanalysis. Why is it that men have provided the theories and knowledge and dominated women in this field? Yatin and Usman came in with their own data keeping a focus on the same question inverted in favour of women. At times women dominate Psychology, like more colleges for women than men or in a limited scenario like Indian Psychoanalysis there are more women than men—they averred. What could be the explanations for the gender differential in Psychology and Psychoanalysis?

I did suggest to Prakriti the unusual direction adopted by

Freud in his choice of bisexuality as the overarching theme, a conception also present in Hindu mythical image of completing male and female modalities as in Ardhnarishwara. No woman or man exists alone for all the deceptive appearances emanating from body forms; rather these are to be looked up as modalities of Sensing and Doing or Feeling and Thinking respectively and reaching blends and varying degrees of fusion in Becoming. Yet to allocate a historical context, I also started looking out for a paragraph to hold the question for future classes since it was already too late. My phone rang. The ringtone must have struck some curious students since it has a piece on violin, hailing the spirit of the lover devotedly joining in words the theme of an old-time Bollywood hero of 1960s, placing his heart in fervent surrender at the feet of his beloved.

Knowing what we now know today, it is obvious that somebody had to come sometime who would decide that it would be better for the sake of the study of human motivation to call too many rather than too few things sexual, and then to modify the hypothesis by careful inquiry. For it was only too easy to do what had become civilization's 'second nature,' that is, in the face of the man's sexual and aggressive drives, forever to beat a hasty retreat into romanticism and religionism, into secrecy, ridicule and lechery. The patients' fantasies were sexual and something sexual must have existed in their early years. Freud later called that something psychosexuality, for it encompasses the fantasies as well as the impulses, the psychology as well as the biology in the earliest stages of human sexuality. (ibid, p. 33)

I knew I was reading to myself and the entire class had moved away into their own fantasies. My effort to get them into the domain of all-inclusive psychosexuality for us to travel towards dreaming, psychic determinism, gender bias, bisexuality etc. was at best that they could inwardly laugh at, and at worst they would openly yawn and slip out. So I stopped after completing my reading saying : 'I know you are not as interested in what I am reading but I ought to complete my steps regardless'. To that many responded with a gentle laugh. So did Surbhi—my closest companion in this class. But to my great astonishment, I found Shreya laughing heartily with tears flowing down gently on her face. Did I get nervous by her tears? Likely. I tried to gain a foothold on the episode of my phone having rung towards the end. I also felt an idiosyncratic confusion return in that moment: mis-calling ringtone as caller-tune. Some students, renewed in their eagerness by the Bumble-bee I had become and Shreya's laughter mixed with tears, wanted me to tell them about the song; others were moving out—too tired of the obsession of being the first. A whole parental generation expects only this from them! Perhaps.

I decided to sing for them just one line of this melody duet sung by Mohd. Rafi and Asha Bhonsle. So I sang in the belief that it would appeal in its underlying register of how mutuality emerges by turns if one succeeds in preserving the music and lilt of life. The song in its opening brings up an arch-tease, thrown in by both the male and female characters at each other (in the wake of deep sentiments of complete surrender as well an unswerving pledge of loyalty): To think separately to attain a future in the life of love. How paradoxical!

Male: *Humne toh dil ko aap ke qadmon pe rakh diya is dil ka kya karenge ye ab aap sochiye.*

Female: *Hum aap ki wafa ki kasam kha rahe hain aaj kaise wafa karenge ye ab aap sochiye.*

It got itself sung well. Except that Vikrant decided to take his steps (qadam), first towards Varuni (with white balloon) and taking it away from her said: Let me take this poor baby (the balloon) out for a walk. And out he went.

A First. A woman student who had tended it in the class throughout. A male student doing his bit to take it out on a walk towards a fresher outside.

The class was over but resumed in me soon as I too went towards my office. Later in the evening, I wrote to these few students about their thoughts so I could write down my first account of a class that became music to my ears. How was it to others'? Some students responded in their own time. Surbhi compared herself to a salad plate placed during weddings that is often ignored whilst people pick up their crockery close enough to it and yet move towards the main dishes. An uncharacteristic expression of identification with edible self whose nutrient value is more often sidestepped. Usman responded by comparing the carnivalesque atmosphere that exceeds people's capacities to go on listening, yet is not unwelcome.

Shreya Bakshi surprised me further by writing her salient thoughts and adding to them a memorable pictogram which I would attach here along with her explanations of it through her mail. I wish to express my gratitude to her in convincing me through this calligraphic painting preserving critical themes of the class, that the class had had an impact on at least one more person, in the process completing the dyad—the essence of Clinical Thinking—the essence of the Clinical First. Not just that she also summoned her own compelling title Fugue. In formulating the final title Fugue to First: Some Movements in the Melody of Empathy, I happily acknowledge her co-authorship to the emotional template of this writing.

Shreya's Explanation of the pictograph:

The title Fugue has been chosen from the Baroque music period. It corresponds to several independent melodies that though begin at different times, retain their harmony. Just like these several independent melodies, we had many distinct events happening in the classroom which were eventually compressed and thereafter harmoniously analysed. One may also refer to these multiple events as chaotic and hence draw reference from 'dissociative fugue' however, the attempts have been made to make this as more of a musical piece (also noting that it was the singing that ultimately closed the class in an equally harmonious way).

The first glance at this artwork may cause some unrest. The reason why I've depicted a skull in this artwork is because of a simple reason: skulls are uninhibited. Since they aren't veiled under a skin, they bare themselves to the beholder. And it is their 'smile' that reminds me of my laugh, an uncontrollable fit, bare and unveiled.

In both the eye sockets, you will some symbols. The first one, a 10 rupees coin, clearly demonstrating Surbhi's challenge in terms of a reinforcer (primary or secondary). The second one, a Psi symbol, representing the discussions around how psychology, in reality is often perceived in a gender biased fashion. (Brought up by Yatin and Prakriti, interestingly, Yatin's initial letter (Y) almost resembles a Psi.

The question mark is symbolic of Madeeha and Usman's questions. Being slightly twisted towards the edges and sometimes disconnected by awkward silences of forgetfulness. The red colour in this, reminds me of Madeeha's statement: "People have never bid goodbyes to me. They have simply left me."

The blue colour that I've used depicts Douglas's need to ask for a water break. The shade of blue being like that of the ocean. Ocean, brimming with salty waters, just like my tears that relentlessly trickled down my cheeks as I laughed heartily.

And to contain all of these together, what all could I think of but a balloon? The helium Balloon that Varuni was carrying became a symbolic sac that was no longer filled with air, but memories.

Moods of the Postpartum: Psychoanalytic Labours

Nearly a year has passed as I am giving final touches to this writing. The moments where "teaching" happens through my physical presence in a group or with an individual, often become so passion laden that my speaking becomes closer to dreaming, to borrow from Thomas Ogden (2009); if I am allowed to take a dig at myself—near-psychotic states drown the precious gems that appear as links in free associations in the first set of expressions. As I sit down to strike another relationship with my memories to renew my friendship with them in order to write, the matrix becomes over-porous. So many other thoughts and issues slip in that I get fatigued in surmounting and retaining a coherence. Must share though: Bits and passages do remain, keeping my hopes high of formulating them to a better level of satisfaction. However, this occasion is turning out to be an incredibly new one. The "melodious" seems to have struck a resourcefulness in me, to not let slip three or four potential notes. Indeed, I need to gather these in with a certain courage, to which my young friends distinctively contributed.

My feeling of being taken aback when I entered the classroom, most of the lights having been switched off except few. Surbhi under a fuller light close to my chair, too close for intellectual task of teaching to go on for a teacher, I have revisited this unfathomable moment number of times. Isn't this dramatization to be rigorously "dissected for its internal meaning" to me, as a Teacher of psychoanalysis, to the oldest person in this program and through me to others as Faculty to this unique program in our country?

Today I can clearly feel an admiration for this student to have overcome impressive norms of propriety, also on behalf of many, to playact with statuesque dignity. She let her body impulsions locate sizzlingly close a complementary unworded equanimity in herself. Rest of the students, especially the vocal ones with their radical questions as well as the ones who repeatedly lost their thoughts, represented the necessary correlates to the task; anxieties of the group lent themselves to commendable questions during the class whilst Usman became symbolic of the necessary goof ups through raising of hand and losing the thought for expressing himself in the same instant! Only a class in psychoanalytic thinking with its unique paraphrase of psychosexuality present in all human endeavours, could have precipitated this cameo, howsoever bizarre for a reader outside. Over time, I have felt more staunchly for this event for its many exhibits of spontaneous moods that adorn grave concerns not confined to the youth alone and help renew the worn-out clichés in our awareness and thinking. A part belonging to of all of us, present in the class that day, went out for a stroll in the white balloon towards the end that day. Up there this part, dancing laterally, perched high in the open air and retaining a secure thread-wrap around the fingers of young Vikrant, it managed to read few forms, inside the "smiling pale yellow skull" drawn below by Shreya.

I have also felt a gratitude towards the unconscious wisdom that brought up in my preoccupations before the class the image of a dead salamander preserved in the School laboratory, wondering to myself how it may have been drawn to questions of the students of old dying on the young, and needing to take charge of not burdening them with abrupt losses. I continue to feel an undefinable curiosity for more diffuse perceptual memories of colors dancing in flames as various chemicals burn in the laboratory of my memories and pristine elements of air light and water are reconfigured ---could this have contributed to that phrase, with megalomaniac tones, "searching for ethics in amniotic fluids"? I know I am also caressing some of these moments before these go out and draw the readers in.

Idioms of a "Laboratory in intersubjectivity" and "Schooling in Method" when faced with various hues of the buried and forbidden, not to misrecognize the foetal found therein, as either complete-new or puckered-old, remain my closing promise to the reader, even as I keep faith in melodic nature of my reveries and Erikson's inimitable coinage of the balance that was accomplished in this method: a new blend of the elements of "feminine intuition, child-like curiosity and artistic freedom of style were recognized and restored as partners of the masculine "inner tyrant" in the process of psychological discovery" (ibid, p. 38).

References

Bolognini, S. (2008). *Secret Passages: The Theory and Technique of Interpsychic Relations*. London: Routledge.

Erikson, E.H. (1964). *Insight and Responsibility: Lectures on the Ethical Implications of Psychoanalytic Insight*. New York: W.W. Norton.

Ogden, Thomas H. (2009). *Rediscovering Psychoanalysis: Thinking and Dreaming, Learning and Forgetting*. East Sussex: Routledge.

20

Between Praxes of Excellence and Pragmatism of Real World

Jatin Bhatt

It is difficult to reflect on something so close as one might not see the experience dispassionately, especially when what one does and what one is, appear to be a unified identity. For the most part, teaching has been a journey of enjoyment and self-actualization. My approach has been based on how I saw my role in developing an enabling environment within an institutional set-up which then, was completely a new experience for me.

The way out to write this essay, I thought, was to reach out to my past students starting from the firsı cohort and subsequent batches I had taught across different institutions. So, I sent out the very brief (in italics below) which I myself had received to my students with a request to send in their perception of me with reference to the brief in about 100 words.

> *This is an invitation to share your experiences of being a teacher, using critical and experiential pedagogical processes, listening to your students, your struggles, successes, failures, your philosophy of teaching, your journeys of walking alongside young lives, your dreams, your imaginative sojourns, your critique of the manner in which teaching and learning is generally practised, moments and figures that inspired you, classroom experiences and attempts to hold your students—the times when this could happen and*

> *when this slipped away. Also write about the voices in your inner theater as a teacher—the fear of being rejected by students, anxiety, eagerness, tension, joy whatever it may have been. To be reckoned with are your attempts to bring the structural and the experiential, the political and the psychic, the conceptual and the emotional to a dialogue in classroom spaces. Your attempts to give space to differences as differences and not to quickly make them into hierarchies also matter*

Of thirty two students I reached out to with a deadline of four days, I had an overwhelming twenty five responses! On reading their responses I was amazed to see the ways in which they remembered me. To know that they hold me in such esteem has been a truly humbling experience. What more can teachers ask for but to be of significance in the lives they have nurtured? I truly consider it my good fortune to have had an opportunity of facilitating my students' growth at some point or other in time. Even if it makes this writing sound like a story of self-glorification, I have chosen to sparingly include a few of their voices in the reflections that follow. Their feedback is the most authentic source, validating my teaching capabilities. In this sense I owe this write-up to my students.

Shrishti, a former student wrote back saying

> My single most vivid memory of you as a teacher was your instinctive understanding of each of your students and using that to prompt individual growth. Your ability to simplify and make everything a matter of fact allowed a very organic thinking process, providing enough space for everyone to arrive at their own conclusions; it did give an open space for all kinds of creative ruminations.

(Shrishti Bajaj now a Course Leader Product Design, Pearl Academy Delhi)

Despite having spent more than twenty years in design academics, I still wonder as to whether I think of myself as a teacher. Considering my involvement in active academics was more a matter of a chance, I find myself with a reasonable following of students who graduated over time during my long innings in design education. Let me share a bit of the history that got me into academics in the first place.

Before getting into academics, I must clarify that my engagement in that field had always been predominantly that of providing academic leadership and management either as a founding Department Chair or as a founding Dean. I have never been one of the many faculty member as seen from the vantage point of students, faculty colleagues or the institutions that I work with except on the rare occasions of my engagement as guest faculty in other institutions. It is natural for students to perceive the position of 'authority' through a different lens.

Closing the Door Open

I wound up my office early evening on 31 December 1990 to prepare for a new year's party that I was hosting. Out of the blue, I got a call from the Executive Director of the National Institute of Fashion Technology (NIFT), New Delhi to attend a meeting on 1 January 1991 to plan a workshop as a precursor to the new department of Accessory Design being planned at NIFT. Running a reasonably settled design consultancy company and not having the slightest inclination towards academics, I told her that she had called up to a wrong person and that I had nothing to do with either fashion or academics. Besides, I was not in a mood to work on the new year's day after a long party. She insisted that I meet her in any case on the following day and that a car would pick me up. Not realizing that the meeting would completely change my course of career and work, I reluctantly agreed.

Still in the mode of denial to be involved in academics, I set out to work on a proposal as a part of my consultancy assignment to develop a framework for a programme and a new department of Accessory Design at NIFT Delhi with no real thoughts on future engagements beyond visualizing the curricular framework and a concept note for the Department. A matter of fact presentation to about twenty experts from various related fields at IIC turned into a passionate position and argument about what I thought the programme focus should be. Considering my shortcomings and lack of experience, I requested that the proposal be evaluated by academics with long-standing experience. It was decided to invite Professor M.P. Ranjan (now late) for a two-day workshop to give it a robust structure with clear rationale that befitted the academic structure and curriculum design.

Managing my practice and chairing the Accessory Design Department that I succumbed to, put me at the crossroads of choosing my future. Did I believe I could add any value to this academic venture? Being at the helm of affairs as it turned out to be in my first encounter with academics, I realized the potential and power to change and influence the design scenario in industry sectors I could not imagine my practice to ever achieve.

A small space carved out of the workshop belonging to the Office of The Development Comissioner (Handicrafts) in an unmaintained ramshackle industry shade in Okhla within the Regional Design and Technical Development Centre (RDTDC) full of frustrated employees was not going to help matters either. Without even a basic canteen and no electricity for most of the day, the programme was fully dependent on a small generator that either supported room coolers or a projector. Dependent on guest teachers with me being the only 'full time' faculty and Chair, it became an everyday orchestration of events that continued to defy the programme timetable. It was a perfect challenge to invigorate the entire situation that could create synergy between potentially enthusiastic students and some highly-skilled but pessimistic artisans.

While it seemed an exhilarating opportunity, students' expectations and attitudes to professional education became the biggest challenge between my imagination and their lackadaisical response. 'How can we work so much?' and 'Why do not you like our work when we put in so much of time?' was the first rebellion by the very first miniscule batch of eleven students. Silent protests, disappearance from classes and poor attendance on the part of the students were not the best start for my academic career. Tentative commitment of the institution management along with continuous criticism and questioning from faculty from other departments watching this new story of my approach and methodology did not help the situation much. Complaints from a few students to the Executive Director about excessive work demands hidden behind the infrastructure (which was extremely basic compared to the posh main campus) issues ensured a sustained tension with the management. In some of the exasperating moments, I also offered to quit if I was not allowed my space for at least two years. 'Yes, my approach is not like other design programmes borrowed from the US, but, since I was invited as an 'expert' by you, you will have to trust me!' I argued. There was some discomfort with an indigenous approach that did not copy similar programmes from the US or Europe. I was convinced that I knew better what would work in the Indian scenario. I do not know if it was arrogance or confidence. Either way, I had no choice but to prove it.

Recalling that time, Aminesh writes:

> He would not handhold, would never offer a straight solution, would never set humanly-achievable challenges (or so I thought then!). All the much despised 'free-wheeling' instilled me with 'Curiosity', an insatiable 'Thirst for Knowledge', 'Confidence' and above all a 'Sense of Being'—the most valuable gifts from a teacher to a student.

(Kirti Oram, Director Melange Design Accessory Design, NIFT Delhi)

> In my experience, the first two years saw a huge dropout rate of around 50% due to students' inability to cope with the demands of the programme in quality outputs and intensity of work expectations. Not many were prepared for an average 10 hours' work day after day. It was disappointing to see some really talented students leave the programme due to work pressure along with a few due to poor performance. In hindsight, such a high level of expectations paid off and created a work culture that even today, is seen as a significant value by the graduates. But that is how the real life work

> culture in design practice is! What started as peer pressure and stories of non-relenting faculty as hard taskmasters from seniors transformed into a more self-motivated engagement with projects and assignments. Before the end-semester juries and graduation shows, the studios and workshops were humming with activities and working through nights became a norm.

The nature of disparate challenges to overcome without losing my larger dream to be realized made my resolve even stronger. It was no more about teaching alone and more of providing the best possible ecology for all involved to develop a passionate sense of engagement and ownership of the space, learning and teaching process, proactive interactions and purposeful encounters within and outside the institutional space. Against this backdrop was a conscious task of '*designing' a process of transformation from being learners to practitioners* within the stipulated programme tenure of the students' journey. This, to me has been the core of my academic brief and larger contribution as a 'teacher'. In a way, it called for developing a work culture that would define the very core of the Accessory Design Department at NIFT.

As Reena recalls,

> I was very pleased with a form I was developing, and clearly remember his reaction on my explorations, saying that I was busy decorating the forms externally but missed out on the finer nuances of what forms could communicate as a whole. He questioned my approach often, making me think deep and push boundaries. I learnt that in all art, what you choose to leave out is no less important than what you include.

(Reena Ahluwalia, Global Consultant Jewellery Toronto First Batch Accessory Design, NIFT Delhi)

> In a functioning fashion institution with much hype and glamour associated with it, this initiative had to be differently grounded, devoid of the frills and yet truly innovative and deeply rooted in appreciating the finer nuances of design as it would be in the real world. That its graduates will be

> thought leaders with ability to transact with real world with confidence, pride and deep-rooted values of ethics in practice. Despite the brief that was overtly limiting and stated as 'Design For Business' to ensure the industry sectors found alignment with their core expectations of design as a business value, underlying premise was more deeply rooted in macro perspectives of opportunities beyond business and industry. NGOs, self-help groups, unorganized sectors and crafts too intersected significantly in the curricular transactions with a deep sense of empathy, mutual respect, humility and a larger societal purpose of Design in practice and concerns.

Early years called for ensuring that the students, faculty colleagues and external entities felt valued. Small but continuous gestures of appreciation of achievements or contributions without losing sight of the larger goals were needed to ensure that all stakeholders were invested in this 'collaborative process.' Especially with students, this was always a difficult phase as any gesture of appreciation would lead them to complacency and subsequent critique or expectations would often get them into regressive mindsets and disengagement from work/assignments. I have continued to visit this challenge time and again where balancing a sense of rejection, encouragement and pushing individual boundaries of students is more an interpersonal skill than mere academic acumen. In a discipline like design rooted in individuality where students passionately own an idea, they truly believe in, 'how do you summarily dismiss it without a deeply felt sense of hurt often leading to self-doubts?' For some students, the sense of momentary hurt gave way to a long-term process of gaining insight into the self. Tshering points towards this in her ruminations:

> Tshering is just going to sit and watch the world go by' seemed an offhand remark coming from Mr. Bhatt during a conversation in some context. Years later as a designer I felt I was unsure of what I was doing and recollected these lines dreading that he may have been right. Now I ask myself this question every time I feel lost. It helps me to take account of

> my work and life in general. At the same time I truly admire the acute observation and analysis that he made of a weak spot in me that l could work upon and still do.

(Tshering Dholkar, Assistant Professor Accessory Design, NIFT Shillong)

Connecting with Life Beyond Education

The sensitivity of students to deal with and overcome rejection became one of the paramount concerns in due course as, it would manifest in real life and practice. This meant that life skills must be an integral part of learning. There had to be differentiation between selling an idea and developing an ability to put forth a compelling argument. With many students being linguistically challenged, it was not about glib talk as it was about clarity of thinking through one's argument, which elucidates thorough insight into the issue/situation at hand. More so, it is about laying bare the realm of possibilities for a well-imagined outcome. I always enjoyed this space of process-driven anticipation, planning and negotiation of multiple probabilities in real-life engagements as a well-honed skill developed over ten years of my consultancy prior to my involvement in academics.

Bhashob gives it words on my behalf:

> I have come to believe that teaching has less to do with ensuring that a student has a knowledge base or appropriate skill set. It is got to do more with enabling an individual to have a 'bent of mind', a way of seeking rightfully. It is about perceiving 'inclinations' specific to an individual and nurturing 'those inclinations' to bloom. It essentially brings out the best in us.
>
> Mr. Jatin Bhatt, whom I have loved immensely and also had the freedom to be equally upset with, contributed to my understanding of not only design, but also the vocation of teaching.

(Bhashob Majumdar, Furniture Design Consultant Bengaluru, Accessory Design, NIFT Delhi)

For a professional programme in Design intended to focus on industry sectors that survived on 'reverse engineering' for product design and development or were churning out more of the same products, it became imperative to educate the sectors dealing with leather goods, jewellery and crafts. Despite their obvious shortcomings in design and product development, they exhibited arrogance and berated the idea of training design professionals who could be of value to them. The industry believed that since they had been into their business for a long while, an undergraduate programme of just three years (it was approved as a two-year programme but was changed in the second year to three years through my protracted arguments with NIFT) as the students could hardly even understand their sector and product challenges.

Industry often treats students and academic institutions with disdain believing that students, faculty and institutions are too insular to have any real understanding of the real world challenges. Internships and projects are seen as a wasteful obligations by the industry with no real gain. At the same time, fresh graduates are expected to be work-ready in the real world. This is more specific to professional or vocational programmes where graduates are expected to perform almost immediately after completing studies. This to me appeared untenable having seen the industry from close during my practice. Rather, the industry itself was completely unfamiliar with Design as an expertise and a function within industry. I was determined to change this and put forth a new challenge for the department to not only transform this perception but also build a synergistic relationship with industry for an innovative academic ecology of the department. This would ensure that industry values Design and our students of design not only as a significant part of their business, but also as real change agents.

In the recalling of Tejmohan:

> As other faculty and departments were determined to implement and enforce a pecking order where they ruled the roost, Mr. Bhatt and his accessory design faculty team, were busy making friends with young minds and getting

> down to our level. By becoming a friend he could tap into our inner selves. He would then understand our core and design a teaching plan to extract the best in us. Demanding he was, but demanded excellence from us not as authoritarian headmaster would, but more like an older brother. Mocking us on our under-par effort on a sketch or a prototype, as he dipped a tea bag a hundredth time into his tea cup, igniting a fire for us to be better than we felt we could ever be.

(Tejmohan Sawhney, BOSKOVS USA Accessory Design, NIFT Delhi*)*

Initiatives in small classroom projects with real-time industry participation in early semesters created just the right challenge, enthusiasm and self-belief among students and provided opportunities to share their approach and process with individual industry clients. It required a hard-nosed relationship building veiled in utmost humility to get small groups of industry to engage in classroom projects. The message was clear; if the students provide what is of value to the industry, then they need to pay for it! These opportunities were used to encourage students to stretch the brief to expand industry imagination. After all, they had to be the thought leaders and change agents who would bring about acceptance and respectability to practitioners of design in the real world.

The graduation projects provided a perfect platform for students to be located at the individual industry sponsor for five months to show their mettle on a brief controlled by respective faculty guides to ensure the quality of work was commensurate with the benchmarks set-up by the department. This was always a tough negotiation to ensure that students got maximum support ecology and funding from the industry. Except for a few rare situations, most industry partners did oblige and in the process got to appreciate design as a process and expertise and not a random spark of ideas. Even now, so many of the industry representatives credit their engagement with these student projects as a moment of a paradigm shift in their understanding of Design. For good many years, these projects were showcased with aplomb in an elaborate Graduation Show with around 500 invitees through sponsorships. These required a month-long preparation from planning to coordination managed largely by almost all students across batches. It became a huge learning process for students of managing a large event of scale and complexity done with utmost quality and care. More than anything else, it was a sense of recognition, appreciation and public display that ensured that students graduated with a 'high'. Multiple opportunities to participate and showcase their work in various trade events in different parts of India during their early semesters helped honing their skills in planning and execution of events.

As Harpreet reminisces:

> Mr. Bhatt has constantly motivated me to seamlessly marry academic learning with realistic application in industry. This learning has not been limited to the finer nuances of the design process and has extended well into the domain of design management, design ethics and professional behaviour. This broad and passionate outlook towards our profession seems to extend very naturally from his warm and amiable persona. Mr. Bhatt can be equally at ease nurturing the childlike curiosity of young design students or fiercely debating design policy with officials and administrators.

(Harpreet Padam, Partner and Designer Unlike Design Co., Accessory Design, NIFT Delhi)

Consultancy projects taken up by the faculty were structured to engage students to get a fair sense of the scale and complexities of challenges they would encounter in their professional life. Hardly any consultancy project was visualized without students' formal involvement. Whether it was a nationwide study of gold jewellery, analysis of Moradabad craft industry, holistic development of Self-Help Group of Muslim women in Salai Gaon UP or post-earthquake rehabilitation of craft communities of Kutch, students were an active part of delivering a well-defined research or design component of these projects with an average timeframe of two years. These projects gave them a critical exposure to the socio-political milieu of the real world. Students were often involved with me in the conceiving of the initial project proposals like setting up of a Toy Design Centre funded by UNODO or a part of significant field studies for developing an online portal as a virtual Centre for Design Management for craft industries. Being a part of client presentations by the faculty gave them a ringside view of large complex projects at different levels of execution and negotiations.

To use Avinash's words:

> Beyond being an artist or a designer of objects and experiences, I learnt something far more fundamental from you—the art of making a proposal—which is really about building bridges between the world and yourself, softening hard realities with the inner world of dreams, and finding resonance in a discouraging world. I have no hesitance in admitting that my professional success and personal growth both owe a great debt to the trust and faith you vested in me when I was just 19! It is a true reminder that education is a platform, not a destination. Thank you!

(Avinash Kumar, Founder Director, Quicksand Design Research Delhi-Bengaluru-Goa, Accessory Design, NIFT Delhi)

Pedagogic processes in Design Education invariably tend to demand a high level of student faculty interaction and transaction at both emotional and intellectual levels. Time spent on each individual student project is almost like a parallel faculty project. Their successes and failures almost become synonymous with faculty predicaments. Young eighteen-year-olds come with varied socio-cultural, economic and family challenges. Their new-found freedom from the regimented school experiences is generally at loggerheads with the disciplinary demands of a professional programme. While many might have rebelled against their parents to pursue such a nonconformist field, some others might have been struggling with broken marriages of their parents. Their relationship with the faculty is both of a demonic figure who would not compromise on expectations and also that of an elder to whom they look up to for addressing their trials and tribulations. They are emotionally vulnerable and yet seek recognition of their individuality. They are ambitious and full of energy but are difficult to be tied down to serious responsibilities. They are in the process of self-discovery where their idiosyncrasies need to be given space for personal growth while developing a sense of mutual respect. Gamesmanship and negotiations with a teacher are seen to be great achievements. Challenging authority is normal and there is a kick out of breaking rules. Failures and reprimand are almost always insulting, and more so in front of others.

Our Disability: Inadequacy of Normalcy

After the notification to enroll students in PWD category, my colleagues and I were in a serious dilemma when a student with hearing and speech disability was to be considered for admission. How would we explain assignments, give feedback or communicate with him without a shared medium of transaction? But then, design can be transacted through tools of drawings or visual instructions. Should we take on the challenge considering it was about an individual's career and our inability to deal with this situation? After some deliberations among faculty colleagues and shared belief, it was decided to enrol him with an interpreter. The interpreter did not work out as the sheer complexity of the courses and full days of classes frustrated the interpreter and us alike. It was then that the issue was put up to his classmates to ensure that they spent extra time with him to explain the daily transactions. It was to the credit of these classmates that not only did he survive the entire programme successfully but also was picked up by a very design-conscious corporate in their design unit designing watches. The entire experience spread over three year was one of the most significant challenges that the faculty team overcame, though with a lot of unusual and innovative methods of transactions. However, not all faculty colleagues were happy with the decision to enrol him in the first place.

Being Invested-Being True: *I care... but no nonsense please*

Students easily recognize your likes and dislikes, consistency, self-image, knowledge, openness, larger values in life, courage of conviction, intellectual honesty, opinions, passion, pride, emotional investment and character. Accessibility, engagement, encouragement, fairness and welcoming demeanour are some of the qualities that attract students to engage with and look up to you. Even then, not all students may connect with you with ease and comfort especially when you happen to be in a position of authority. Emotional trauma of failures, broken relationships or conflicts with parents that students often wanted me to deal with, required sensitivity, empathy, advice and a dispassionate approach to help them face the reality and overcome such impediments. Often, issues involved parents and their anxieties about workload, programme and future prospects. Rare occasions were also there about questioning of the evaluation process by parents, especially the ones holding high government offices, when their wards failed the semester. These were trying times for me being at the helm as any such decision was ascribed to me. Fortunately, all other students rallied around the process of evaluation and its inherent objectivity. This sense of conviction and self-belief emanated from the students as captured in Bhavna's poetic recollection:

> HE-who looked authoritative, yet, calm
> who ruled my design world, yet, set me free to dream, beyond rules
> who sent terror down my spine, yet, the one to back me up, as if his own
> who tested me in hot waters, as if to mould me, into who I am
> who supported me and solved my problem, with just a call
> who sounded like the big boss who could throw me with a toss,
> but, only to ensure, I land all the way across
> who taught me to trust my decisions and plunge........plunge...
> to learn, to float, to swim and to set my course.

> This is to-a mentor, a facilitator, a guru, a teacher, a role model, an educator, a fighter, a visionary, a creator, a life changer, an advisor, a pillar of strength, a diving board or a launchpad only to soar.....
> Today, I stand tall and I think, I know it all... It is because of HIM.
> 'He' who kindled the flame, educated my mind and heart, and showed me where to look.
> To him 'I' owe, OWE it ALL!!!! Thank you for making me STAND this TALL.

(Bhavna Yadav, MA Education USA, Accessory Design, NIFT Delhi)

In early years, many of my graduates routinely sought my advice on issues of new employments, career paths, new ventures and challenges of practice. Even after being well-settled and having gone places within India and outside, the relationship continues. I treat them more as friends and often join them over food or drinks. They share their stories of work and life and include their spouses who I am told, are bored of their stories about me. Some of them are very close to my family. A few of their parents have become and remain so my family friends more than fifteen years after we first met. Are these a part of a teacher's contribution I wonder? While this adulation is always gratifying, I am just doing my job with a dream they are a part of.

My long stay with NIFT where I was initiated into academics, ended abruptly on a disappointing note. I put in my papers within a day of a seemingly planned manoeuvre on the part of the Director General to slight me on some flimsy grounds of propriety. In any case, the overall institutional culture had started to deteriorate even earlier with politicization and new power equations.

Let's Talk—A Way of Immersion

> As a student, I never felt that teaching ever happened in Prof. Jatin Bhatt's class; it was always an interaction, a discussion

> that was initiated. It was learning through dialogues. The pedagogies that he uses in his teaching today still reflect the same philosophy of learning through discussions and critical, analytical thinking. His way of focusing the discussions on non-obvious issues engages the students in the holistic process of design.

(Krity Gera, Assistant Professor, MDes Industrial Design, SPA Delhi)

Apart from NIFT, I have had the opportunity to be a guest faculty at the MDes Industrial Design Programme of the School of Architecture and Planning Delhi for around seven years. This emerged as an opportunity during my being involved as an external jury member on the final projects of the MDes students. My observation about the projects and the programme devoid of a larger worldview and serious research resulted in a course called 'Seminar'. It was an exciting opportunity to explore larger concepts of Value and Quality pertaining to design.

The course also explored areas of services, informal economies and 'social design'. Students in a Master's programme with architecture background needed a different approach to be engaged in such intangible explorations of themes, much as they were used to respond in material dimensions. Elaborate discussions, presentations and short and long assignments were not only about exploring themes but also about individual instincts and sensibilities of the students as experiential being put forth with passion. I am still connected with many of the students much after their graduation though I met them for two hours a week for only one semester.

Just to recap on my first and the longest involvement in academics:

Education in a formal set-up is not a one-person show. Already into the first year of the programme dependent largely on guest faculty, it became equally urgent to get fellow colleagues into the journey. Putting together a team of imaginative, competent, passionate and ambitious faculty called for identifying and aggressive canvassing of the endeavour over initial years was the key to creating a conducive learning environment. More importantly, each one of them needed to be sharing a common vision while being a strong personality with multiple ideas of pedagogic processes and approach. A small team of five people put together in the first three years with diverse strengths, fiercely protected positions, distinct inclination to specific aspects of curriculum and departmental roles hugely enriched the learning experiences of the students. Highest benchmarks of expectations, a strong sense of excellence in outcomes with nurturing of individuality of students' capabilities with high ethical values became the core characteristic of the department. Such was the commitment and collective ownership of the programme that when the management turned down the request for Rs. 50,000 for the graduation show of the first batch, all department faculty requested for a loan from NIFT to be deducted in one year from the faculty salary. A ten-minutes audio-visual programme on students' work in the graduation project before a big time ramp show of fashion design students completely floored the entire audience of about 700 at the Siri Fort Auditorium. This was a paradigm shift as the students were very reluctant to take up their Graduation Project in an industry believing that it was their last chance to show their creativity, as they believed that industry would stifle their imagination. This assumption stemmed from other design departments set-up prior to Accessory Design Department and had ramp shows of garments designed almost without any constraints.

It was a tough negotiation to convince students that if they believed in what they learnt in the programme, they could excel as imaginatively in their work even within industry constraints. After all, there was no getting away from the real world. The ten-minutes audio-visual show proved a point beyond doubt for not only the graduating batch but also for the subsequent batches who witnessed the adulation and appreciation. From then on, from being an unknown entity in NIFT and outside, everyone was in awe of the Department and students. It had arrived! The next decade saw it grow in stature and influence in industry, research and consultancy projects addressing many industry sectors such as watches, footwear, lighting, architectural accessories, and bathroom accessories. The other impacted sectors were toys and games, visual merchandising, furniture, cane and bamboo, ceramics, jewellery, home décor products, stainless steel, crafts and more in form of product design, community development, self-help groups, skill development, cluster development, livelihoods, customer research, trends research and forecasting, training, design management, projects strategies and sector development.

Engaging with Education Ecosystem

After NIFT, I started an institutional consultancy and apart from designing curricula for new programmes, I got involved with the holistic institution-building of the Indian Institute of Gems and Jewellery at Jaipur. The brief started with a project proposal to the National Skill Development Council to get funding and included overall positioning strategies, programmes development, transaction methods, and faculty training and finally getting on board suitable leadership.

It was a different challenge to engage the existing faculty through actual programme development and use these interactions as an integral part of faculty development. Such a collaborative approach on involving the faculty team in the finer nuances of the programme helps create passionate engagement and ownership along with confidence to deliver the programme with clarity and conviction. It invariably is a slow process akin to educating and training students and in this case, was conducted over two years or so.

Just after leaving NIFT, I got an interesting assignment for curriculum development for a programme on Styling and Image Design, essentially an intangible space, unlike my past experience of design for tangible outcomes. Also, it had no existing precedence or reference. This, I believe was a precursor to give me confidence about MDes Social Design Programme at AUD with similar challenges. It had little precedence and was in the realm of design of intangible outcomes.

The above phase of consulting ensured exciting challenges and gainful engagement. But it could not be a substitute for the complete immersion required to truly guide and influence the finer nuances that characterize the very identity and character of what I intended to achieve. Being a consultant and an outsider in academics with little control of the complex dynamics of education, the sense of gratification was missing.

It was during the year 2012 that I received a call from the Vice Chancellor of AUD requesting me to be on the Selection Committee for Design Faculty for the School of Design. My discussions with Professor Vijaya Varma to visualize the framework of the School prior to faculty selection tempted me to get involved in some manner. It seemed to be a very exciting and unusual brief coming from a university and the perfect challenge to take up the leadership in this endeavour. Given the limitations I had experienced as a consultant and advisor, I chose to go the whole hog into it.

Among Dreamweavers and Heretics

Working in a university has been completely a new experience for me. My initial experiences of the discussions within disciplines of Social Sciences and Humanities were of a mixed sense of intrigue and familiarity. Despite connecting with them through my past exposures both through readings or discussions as a generalist that all design professionals are, the very intensity, depth and the jargon were overbearing. Meetings of the Senior Management Team and Standing Committee for Academic Programmes at Ambedkar University Delhi helped in better appreciation of the disciplines through various programmatic exposures. One distinct difference I noticed was the preoccupation with research and peer recognition through publications and paper presentations. While the discipline of Design is about proactive engagement with real issues to demonstrate change through material and societal engagement, many social science disciplines appeared to be seated on the fence preoccupied with critique and little real-time immersion. It seemed like, if you do not know Heidegger, Foucault, Derrida, Freud or Marx and the likes enough, you have no place in a university. My subsequent exposure to and interaction with the faculty colleagues, programmes, centres and schools helped in sorting out these seemingly discomforting conflicts between Design and other disciplines.

If Design is subsumed and lacks a clear identity within a university, students too will face a similar challenge of being marginalized in the nature of discourse that obtains within a university environment. In that sense, I also found myself out of my comfort zone within the School of Design. MDes Social Design Programme was the very challenge, which got me interested in joining AUD in the first place. A new imagination of a design programme with hardly any similar initiatives can only be tested through actual implementation. While the programme has matured through periodic restructuring and corrective iterations based on the students' experiences and faculty reflections, it has been a significant challenge to establish the efficacy of the programme among the early batches of students. Popular imagination of Design as it prevails among university fraternity still continues to be a work in progress. More so, as Design is seen and perceived to be in the domain of objects, products and material manifestation among people at large. A programme like Social Design is nowhere close to the expectations and understanding of the discipline of Design. It is a peculiar situation in which all constituencies including students, faculty, other colleagues in the university and the larger outside world are still in the process of making sense of the programme focus.

A large part of reaffirming my conviction about the value of the programme has been through sustained engagement with students. That the graduates will open up the potential alignment with real-world issues is hugely dependent on advice, mentoring and guidance of students to seek, identify or create opportunities for themselves.

My aim was as Bhabesh says:

> I have not only learned academically but also learned important lessons in life. Your methods of tackling conflicts inside and outside classrooms, between students or between student and teacher allowed me to see and understand

different perspectives in life or an event. Also I learnt to respect these perspectives no matter how different they might be from mine. In your class you allowed our difference and different opinions, on the topics you taught, to flourish and also helped us evolve them in the right direction. You stuck with us not only in highs but also during our lows, supported and encouraged us not to quit.

(Bhabesh San San Wal, MDes Social Design, AUD)

I do believe that if Design as a discipline is a part of a university, it must have a visible presence of its existence in physical, experiential and academic dimensions. That while Design is distinct in its character, identity and manifestation and yet connects with larger social, cultural, economic and political nuances that are in the larger realm of Social Sciences is something that needs to be taken note of.

My own struggles after graduation were similar to ones that students are encountering as Design as a discipline; though it was hardly understood in the outside world in late the seventies, it would not be an argument, which students necessarily relate to.

I am sure that support and guidance will need to be extended to students well beyond their graduation. Simultaneously, concerted efforts will need to be made to orient and engage potential clients and employers of such an expertise, which does not have any precedence. These to me are larger responsibilities of a 'Teacher' and the nature of relationships and confidence between students and faculty need to be on the foundation of long-term support and holistic mentoring.

As in my past academic engagement, I seem to feel a sense of concern about students, way beyond their tenure in the School. Preparing the students to be ready for uncertainties in the real world as an integral part of conversations with students within and outside the formal programme engagement is crucial. I seem to assume these larger concerns in my interactions with the students and like any other teacher, get a great kick out of every student's success.

It is yet early days for the MDes Social Design Programme to be assessed with reference to success of the graduates. But Accessory Design graduates have gone places in their influence and achievements in and beyond the field set out through the programme. A large number of them are either entrepreneurs in design consultancy or brand owners and manufacturers of watches, footwear, jewellery, crafts, furniture, toys, lighting, interior products and more. Others are employed in leading strategic positions in retail, branding, marketing, buying, business promotion, CSR, design and product development, IT and sourcing as directors or lead strategists. Many of them have taken to academics in leading design institutes in India and abroad. Some have been engaged with NGOs and development agencies in areas of social concerns or initiating their own commitments for public good.

In addition to pushing the boundaries of Design and expanding its potential in non-material domains of services, systems, processes and structures, the current practice of Design needs to be equally valued. Only when the entire canvas of the discipline is fully manifested in the School can the true appreciation of the disciplinary expanse and the seamlessness between established practice and imagination and new Design paradigms such as MDes programme be truly valued by all constituents within and outside the University.

It is through Design that the hands, the heart and the mind find unified meaning and proactive engagement with societal concerns.

21

Metamorphosing from a Caterpillar into a Butterfly

Learning and Teaching in the Indian Medical Education System

Sugandha Gupta

As the invitation to write a piece on teaching came my way, I thought it would be useful to reflect on how the Indian medical educational system treats the teacher-pupil dyad. In my initial musings, I started by wondering if there was indeed anything of distinction in medical education from other streams of learning. With time, as my introspection progressed and memories surfaced, I felt a deep need to write on the teacher-student relationship in medical training.

At the outset, I would wish to discuss why the Indian medical education curriculum (MBBS) is considered to be one of the toughest in the world. This is partly due to the number of subjects, and also the vastness and duration of the programme. Most importantly, this system of knowledge transmission carries an implied and universally perceived sense of responsibility. As medical students, we are made to feel that every word one reads, every biopsy specimen one mounts on a microscope, every bacteria or virus one cultivates in the lab, and each cadaveric dissection one performs, will determine our skill, judgement and ability to be helpful to patients and their families. The moment we step inside the gates of a medical institution, we feel the aura of a humongous responsibility that we would carry in our psyche and soul for a lifetime.

Under this tremendous pressure, some students buckle and leave the course right at the outset and some close to midway, some dissociate their anxieties by adopting a strict scientific stance to the learning situation, and others sublimate by empathetically connecting to patients. Still others act out by pursuing a 'devil-may-care' approach that makes them disengaged from their education. In my observation, each student finds himself/herself moving from one of the above defensive patterns to another across the various stages of the training programme. To complete the medical school curriculum is indeed a tough call. This difficult journey is enabled by teachers (almost akin to gurus) who help transform the student—a tender, delicate egg into a beautiful, colourful and confident butterfly by protecting it through the stages of a voraciously 'appetite-d' larva and magically cocooned chrysalis/pupa. So, before I share my own experiences as a teacher in facilitating this metamorphosis, I wish to recollect my 'becoming a butterfly', as this is the pivotal association which helps me to navigate even today through the challenging routes of the tedious maze—the student's mind.

As an 'egg' in the very nascent stages of development, I remember feeling comfortable in the external shell composed of the germinating energy of a new life form. Despite this, I also was quite conscious of the brittleness and fragility of my external shell. This translated into a feeling of apprehension. Metaphorically, I felt something like a tiny sapling who was expected to quickly bloom into a strong tree. This tree was to bear juicy and rich fruits for others to relish. So, the first professional year was simply about acclimatization, springing offshoots and pushing through some roots of my own to stand tall in times to come. The apprehensive attitude of students like me was dealt with by a non-indulgent and stiff unemotional response by most teachers. This meant that seating around a cadaver and dissecting the layers of a formaline-stained, pungent, shrivelled, darkened, contracted dead body, was not to be experienced as a life-altering event but maybe something as commonplace as peeling an onion. Eventually, the teacher's hard external front made us realize that even if we complained, cried or felt afraid, we still had to push through and succeed. What then seemed as ruthlessness, lack and failure of the teacher's ability to empathize with the plight of a nervous student was over time to be appreciated as an experienced foreboding of what was to come. In the student's consciousness it got ultimately registered as a well-mastered stroke that prevented many a faint-hearted novice from buckling under.

The larval stage (second professional year) was about growing, feeding on knowledge (voraciously) and finding strength in self. Building on the first year's learning, now stunning a live frog and dissecting it were not as chilling and challenging a task as it could have been. The second professional year was more about laboratory work. The subjects being:

(i) Pathology—this included segregating a tumor tissue from an individual's body, mounting it on slides and discerning the types of cancerous cells and features of malignancy.

(ii) Microbiology—examining fecal and urine specimens and investigating them for all kind of pathogens—bacteria, viruses, fungi.

(iii) Pharmacology—study of medications, their chemical structure, effects, side-effects etc.

So this year was all about dissociating the body from the disease and imbibing the skill to limit oneself to the observation of a diseased part or a causative agent. The diseased part was not considered in relation to the whole human being. In spite of the second year curriculum being mundane and routine the teachers made efforts to evoke our interest in each of the above-mentioned subjects. They patiently taught us the art of challenging our limits. They fed us more and more knowledge, infusing sources of strength we would need in the upcoming years. Needless to explain, the second professional year lasted eighteen months rather than the usual twelve.

The pupa stage (third professional year) was about preparation for the final stage. This included formation of the skeleton and shaping up the new body parts inside the cocoon.

If the second year was about breaking up the body, organ systems, illnesses into parts, the third year was about putting everything together and deducing the bigger picture (like a jigsaw puzzle). Now anatomy (the structure), physiology (the function), pathology (the illness), microbiology (the causative agent) and pharmacology (medication) were all combined together as we learnt about ophthalmology (visual disorders) and eye, nose and throat disorders etc.

What the teachers taught us now was empathy! They emphasized on an ability to feel for the patient as being a whole person and not just a diseased part or malfunctioning body organ. We were taught to look at the patient as a being bearing a healthy body, a life full of experiences, a past and a future, a family and a purpose. The teachers taught us covertly the art of shouldering the responsibility of evaluating and treating the patient as such. This learning could not have been transmitted though strictness or hardness. So the teachers were now different! When they scolded us for making a wrong diagnosis or for not choosing the best medication, we could sense the worry about the patient in their voice. We ended up following their strict demands of spending more time with the patient and being gentle in our physical examination. We realized these were not unjust teaching demands or a perfectionist streak in the particular persona of our teachers but were their attempts at teaching us the highly valued and extremely important nuances of medical education.

And then came the final stage of liberating the butterfly! The year was devoted to a holistic integration of a student's physical, mental, emotional and social selves so that one would become competent to understand the patient more fully. Examining and treating a patient of stroke did not just mean a physical examination of the limp arm and leg, but also his lived sense of the illness. This included evaluating and understanding his past, his lifestyle, relating to his family, his work and his personality. All of these were important to get a sense of his challenges as well as to visualize his recovery as fully as could be done. And to do this, the teacher and the student became one—envisioning the patient with the same vision, absorbing him with the same attention, touching him with the same tenderness and examining him with shared knowledge. In many moments now, teaching and learning were experienced as a divine connection, infused with mutuality. Adding to the beauty of the work, in several instances during this phase, the patient became the teacher more than one's professors or seniors. The teacher in the patient was the living being who was opening himself, sharing himself, trusting the other and in that manner, teaching each student much more than what the books or teachers could teach. By surrendering their selves to our care, our patients taught us the virtues of trust, responsibility, truth, faith, hope, passion and above all, unison of beings in opposing roles to fulfill a destiny. Our patients were our teachers who created a truly symbiotic relationship. It was our relationship with them from where we discovered our true, vibrant colours of being a butterfly and having beautiful wings. It was with them that we learnt to flutter our colourful wings and to finally fly on our own.

Getting into the shoes of those you respect and hold in awe is as flattering as it is confusing. I remember (with some embarrassment) my initial days of non-formal teaching to be reeking mildly of some conceitedness, misplaced self-valuation and over-indulgence in the role. That being infrequent (thankfully), I got the chance to teach formally as I reprised the role during my three-year-tenure at a teaching post in the Army Medical College at Delhi. My task here was to familiarize a batch of hundred young butterflies (doctors), who were just beginning to break through the chrysalis stage, with some splashes of colours of my own subject—psychiatry. Amongst the many other exciting and predictable clinical streams of medicine, neurology, surgery, gynaecology, orthopedics and more, psychiatry is often an overlooked, underestimated and unsought stream of medicine. Suffice it to say, teaching such a subject was justifiably expected to be an uphill task.

I took strength in my role as a teacher by reconnecting to my past, especially as a final year student of medicine. I recalled two kinds of teachers who had left a lasting impression on me—the first were the ones who made the colours of their subject more vibrant, more wild and sometimes even a little vulgar; they added drama and thrill to the sketch, infusing them deeper for longevity. The second were the ones who merged in their hues so inconspicuously that they blended pale. The latter's teachings hid in the deepest recesses of our minds with no conscious knowledge to ourselves. They stayed there quietly, shining through only when particular hibernating muscles in the dormant parts of our brains were flexed. Sitting and ruminating at the crossroads from being a student to becoming a teacher, I found myself considering the virtues of both kinds of teachers. Both approaches to teaching seemed useful and meaningful. The dilemma was, which kind would I choose to be!

In speaking of teaching, Benjamin Franklin said very aptly—'Tell me and I forget, teach me and I remember, involve me and I learn!' Hence, I tried to teach depression and anxiety disorders as states to be identified with; these were states which were like an exaggerated extension of our usual self in times of despair and threat, respectively. I spoke to students about how the expected sadness of not faring well in an examination could extend to a depressive phase if persistent stressors and a non-supportive external milieu kept on exacerbating and maintaining the pain. And then we tried to imagine the extent of our sorrow when the calamity was as big as having lost a loved one or when one was undergoing a life-threatening trauma. I tried to teach them phobias by thinking about the mild apprehension that most people go through when seeing a lizard on the wall; for some, we discussed this could turn into a state of severe anxiety. Discussions on such matters would be stimulating and assuring of longevity. While talking about disorders like psychosis to students I needed detailed case studies to make a mark which would not only intrigue them but also left deeper imprints in their minds.

In my understanding, it is not just the script or the actors or music or lyrics that convert a feature film into a blockbuster. It is the apt timing of that feature's presentation, the judgement of the need of the audience, their mood, expectations and associations in those moments which give a film the extra edge. So before every class, every clinic, this would be my agenda—feeling the mood, the tiredness hanging over from the preceding prolonged lecture, the nervous energy for an upcoming examination, the jubilation and excitement over the annual fest or the lusting after the forthcoming vacation, a correct judgement, a change in chameleon's exterior and voila—you have a blockbuster. But I asked myself, is it just entering the five hundred crore rupee club that is a declaration of the feature presentation's success? No; I believe not! As I see it, it is when another director says he wants to make a movie like yours—that is success! For me, the success of being a teacher has been that a few of my students (four out of hundred in each batch) chose psychiatry as their specialty in serving humanity for the rest of their lifetime. The fact that four students chose psychiatry over scores of other more ambitious medical streams has been a validation of my teaching being.

The relationship between a teacher and student is indeed complex, more so when you are a teacher who creates space for emotions and experiences to be shared. This readily generates an expectation in the student that you are accessible not only as a teacher but as someone who would be willing to listen with care and empathy. Often, I have found students walk up to me after a class to talk about their phobias or insomnia. At other times, the need was conveyed through questions in lectures which reflected that something personal and disturbing was both being conveyed and also held back. Those were the more challenging instances. It induced in me ambivalence—Should I reach out or wait for the student to come and share? The dilemma used to continue to occupy my mind even outside the classroom space. During such times I used to wonder what my role as a teacher entailed, was it only to teach, was it to leave open space or was it to mother the child, absorbing his/her unsaid needs and gratifying his/her unsought expectations? Mostly it was time and opportunity that presented me with some solution in such situations. However I cannot say that I have reached anywhere close to my potential in extending myself to students beyond the classroom space.

The dictates of the larger system tell my mind to be 'just a teacher' by the book. The 'inner child' and human in me wants me to do more, to cross the defined lines of teaching and to explore it as a relationship. Yet sometimes I tend to hold back my spontaneous yearnings for fear of exposing and invoking vulnerability in the other and also myself. The uncertainty of the outcome in such situations induces a sense of apprehension in me.

Today I do not formally teach. Still I try to have a continuing discussion on the implications of being a teacher with those of my colleagues and peers who are pursuing teaching. I am keen to learn, how they see the teacher-student relation in the medical educational system. Do they think of it only in the literal sense of the word or does it entail anything more for them? I share my experiences with them and prod them to share theirs. One of the things that I have learnt through such interactions, which is of pertinence to medical teaching is that more often than not, it is the 'inner child' with her spontaneous wish to connect that wins. More often than not, a teacher reaches out beyond his/her conventional roles. Probably there is an implicit understanding that to teach a medico covertly, one surely needs the skill to empathize. Also, the tendency to attend to relational concerns stems from long years of interacting with sick people and their families. This has resulted in a situation where most doctors as teachers expand their roles beyond the conventional definitions. And even though, there are no randomized control trials to measure the same, whatever discussions I have had with my peers, there does seem to be unanimity that such an attitude and approach has helped to raise better students—doctors who are more involved with their patients, doctors who are more empathetic and doctors who are keener to continue the pursuit of learning. On my part, I have deeper satisfaction as a teacher whenever I have been able to reach out beyond the conventional teaching definitions.

> Most people are mirrors reflecting moods and emotions of the times, few are windows bringing light to bear on the dark corners where troubles fester; the whole purpose of education is to turn mirrors into windows! —*Sydney J Harris*

22

Critical Education and the Fostering of the 'Bad' 'Mad' 'Maladjusted' Subject

Mamatha Karollil

Seven years ago when I first came to Delhi to start a new life as a teacher at a university, my real estate agent told me reassuringly that I did not have to worry, that as a university teacher and as a South Indian, landlords would be happy to have me as a tenant. According to him, there were four categories of people who had to worry: single people, Kashmiris, Muslims and Punjabis. Even though I belonged to the one of those groups (single), I soon realized that being a South Indian and a 'lecturer' compensated, conferred respectability, and saved me from disrepute and bad citizenship. Last week, a colleague and friend told me that times had changed, that this site of diagnosis of the bad inadequate disruptive citizen, and those arbiters of tenancy that dictated who got to occupy which spaces and neighbourhoods in the city, had discovered another candidate for the black list— University professors.

The new discovery brought back to my mind the frenzied upheaval and protest of the university community following the death of the Dalit scholar Rohit Vemula in early 2016 where for the first time on the streets, those of us possessive of the bodily hexis associated with urban Indian academics/intellectuals/progressives faced hostility, we were read as 'anti-nationals'. What is it about universities of repute in India that they seem to provoke the aggressive attention of the State and the public in these times? JNU, Jadavpur University, Tata Institute of Social Sciences, and Hyderabad Central University are some that have notably become sites of this struggle for legitimacy. Such attention and attempts at regulation find myriad routes: disruption of talks and seminars, various forms of threat and intimidation of teachers and students, attempts at regulating and standardizing syllabus content, stipulating 'links with industry' as a criterion of quality, cuts in funding and attempts at dismantling programmes and centres that deal with social exclusion and social justice such as women's studies centres and Dalit studies centres. What is it about the identity/ subjecthood of the teachers and students in these universities or in these programmes, what is it about their speech and writing, and what is it about their relation to themselves and the world, which provoke anxieties in parents, in the public, and in the State?

When a ruling party parliamentarian says that students of a premier university in the country are wasting tax payers' money to participate in 'protests in the morning' and to smoke cigarettes, dance around fires and have sex by night, joining in this sense of outrage are a range of voices— typically of middle-class, bourgeoisie, vocal minority on social media, and across the country. These assertions provide us with a hint of the answer to that question.

The swiftness of the shared awakening of recognition seems to expose what was a brewing crisis in legitimacy— of what counts as education, who is the ideal teacher, and who is the ideal student. One view of education is that of it preparing change agents who question the status quo: those who see the world as systems of domination and oppression and attempt to articulate ways of negotiating with that world to democratize relations. If that be so, is understandable that those comfortable with the status quo, typically those in power and of power, experience anxiety and a desire to protect the status quo. Following this logic, as someone noted wryly, provoking anxiety in centers of power is the clearest indication that universities claiming to impart critical education are indeed doing so.

The 'feminist', the single woman, the queer, the Dalit, the intellectual, the secularist, the left-liberal, may all be imagined as products of a critical liberal education—whether in the classroom or the streets, the commune—and one and all of them are considered 'bad subjects', with limited citizenship. They have all been the subjects of heightened hostile targeting in recent times—by landlords, the anonymous hecklers (usually young men) on the street who target 'JNU types', the police who confront and threaten youngsters in public parks with arrest or calls to parents, and the right-wing strongmen that target various forms of organizing, protest and expression by these 'bad subjects'. Some figures, and some speech and expression/action simultaneously threaten the narrowly defined sacred imaginaries of identity, family, the good life, prosperity and development, the nation, and history. From them come political assertions and (sometimes fractured)solidarities of myriad forms- as conscience-keepers bending critical reflection on society- for 'other' notions of development, of merit, of division of labour in private and public, of affinity and community. It may be noted that the sites of political action of these 'bad' subjects range across those typically associated with politics (e.g. legal, policy or institutional spheres) to those associated with politics (the interpersonal and kinship spheres).

The anxieties of those in, of and with power are but one side of this problem we are approaching; it describes the macro political-contextual dynamics through which these subjects come to be. When the focus shifts to the structure, relations and dynamics of one of the micro sites of the production of these subjects—the classroom or other University spaces—this throws up other kinds of questions that I believe are relevant to us as educationists. Leaving aside the evident and well-known efforts towards equity, access and a discrimination free milieu for education, leaving aside the politics of knowledge production and dissemination (for whom, by whom and for what purposes), what I wish to focus on is the fostering of 'bad subjects' in places of critical liberal education via critical pedagogy of the self and other.

'Bad subjecthood' as we know from feminists, queer theorists and anti-psychiatrists such as Phyllis Chesler and Jane Ussher (mad women), Michel Foucault (the mad, the criminal, the homosexual), Thomas Szasz and RD Laing (the mad), Judith Halberstam and Sara Ahmed (the queer) may be seen as embodying critique—of the very systems through which they come to be. These theorists variously see such subjects as embodying perfectly 'normal responses' to an 'abnormal world', as personifying resistance to efforts at regulation and/ or as the constitutive other of the normative world. Judith Halberstam in the 'Queer Art of Failure' points to the radical potential that failure presents in a world that defines success in ways that affirm the heteronormative or where it is defined by capital, patriarchy and white aesthetics—marriage and family, big cars and big homes, fancy vacations, the right education and qualifications. Such an interpretation of 'failure'- of the mad, the unemployed, the inarticulate, the uncool, the strange, the forgetful, the difficult, the lazy or the stupid, offers a tremendous scope for self—reformulation for those subjects who heretofore have experienced themselves as less than or have found no language of dignity to describe themselves.

Here we may begin to see how some of these states of being are articulations borne of coming close to the real relations of power and of becoming alive to these. Perhaps these represent, as anti-psychiatrists claim, the breakdown of defences that are crucial to 'healthy functioning': the careful unseeing, the closely guarded, deeply buried vault of memories of humiliations, mortifications, and other forms of self-annihilation. All of these may be imagined as preparing the subject for well-adjusted happy participation in a life-world that favours the powerful and are made in their image. What happens when the basis of this stable world are threatened. Gergen in the Saturated Self speaks of the condition of multiphrenia in modernity, of a self caught between multitudes of potentials and rationalities, of not having the clear and singular certainties that were anchors in tradition, finds itself in states of disquiet, anxiety and lassitude. Thus laziness, paralysis and depression, may also be the symptomatic expression of *resistant* subject facing the painful, if potentially liberating disintegration of familiar and oppressive modes of being and relating. Anger, contrariness and aggression in relationships at work and at home may be the first consequences of the recognition of the oppressive nature of social relations.

Such an understanding of 'failure' hints at the casualties and hazards that accompany a consciousness-raising project such as that is imagined via critical feminist and queer pedagogies. In simple terms, if 'good subjecthood' enlists one into structures of power relationships or systems of oppression, either as the oppressor or the oppressed, if 'false consciousness' masks oppression and political awakening empowers one on the one hand, on the other hand, this process of awakening will also necessarily be painful, disorienting and with the potential for breakdown, for outbursts and sustained, unbearable feelings of rage and outrage.

As educators, this presents a moral conundrum that needs to be thought through. This conundrum spins on the twinned nature of places of critical education that is at once within a dominant social order and presents a critique of it. Such a critique, as educationists note can only arise from such places of knowledge production and dissemination being accommodative of difference, among teachers and students. However the very heterogeneity informs an aspect of the problem. Every student in the classroom has the potential to be touched by critical pedagogy that pushes them to confront the power-riven bases of their existence, both immediate and remote, in micro and macro realms. The classroom and the university, in particular, presents a world where via a new definition of the self, the other and the self in relation with the other, a new social ordering is imagined and embodied. Indeed, students may find themselves in a world where 'bad subjecthood' becomes a mode of being that is for the first time in their lives perhaps, valid and legitimate. Equally, becoming aware of one's complicity in power relations, of the oppressive bases of one's 'good subjecthood', could present students with difficult choice. However, these are choices that they are differently enabled to pursue.

To elaborate: if every student in the classroom or university has the potential to be touched by critical education and if the consequences can be both liberating and painful, some by virtue of their social positioning are better equipped to deal with the implications of such knowledge. Some students, usually privileged by class, caste or gender can bear the costs of 'failure' or bad subjecthood in a manner different from those less privileged who have to confront structures they are powerless to change or escape. Year after year, as some of us critical educationists witness, we come across students who speak of the 'schizophrenia' (as one called it) produced by the world that AUD represents and the ones they return to every evening. These students find themselves in the peculiar bind of recognizing injustice in the norm but yet not having the power or resources enough to bear the costs and risks that accompany the pursuit of non-normative forms of being, loving and working in the world. So one question for educators may be: where 'bad subjecthood' is idealized, in a context that is so antithetical to the normal world 'outside', what are the hazards or casualties of this process that young people face and that we as critical educationists need to think more about?

I would like to end this essay with some thoughts that are yet incomplete. It concerns the question of what new directions a critical education can provide where old ways of being and relating in the world are threatened. The American author Gloria Jean Watkins better known by her pen name bell hooks talks of the absence of the ethics of love in the doing of many forms of politics. The recognition and channelling of anger, the evocation of outrage are useful tools for marshalling effort directed at demolishing or overthrowing systems of power; this is indeed the strategy in trade union politics, caste politics, and certain forms of queer and feminist politics. Hooks raises questions about the place of love, empathy compassion in the forging of a political vision and of building solidarities. Love based as it is on empathy and continuity between the self and other seems antithetical to a politics based on difference. There is the danger of identifying with one's oppressor. Yet, are there ways in which an imagination of commonalities between individuals and groups can coexist alongside recognition of difference? Could these then become the basis of new forms of community and sociality for a young person already in the process of forging a sense of self and the other?

Section 6
Through the Rear View Mirror: Reminiscences of Teachers in Becoming

True teachers are those who use themselves as bridges over which they invite their students to cross; then, having facilitated their crossing, joyfully collapse, encouraging them to create their own.

— Nikos Kazantzakis

Photo credit: Shyam B. Menon

23

Being a Teacher

Witnessing Transformation

Anita Ghai

> We do not learn from experience...we learn from reflecting on experience.
> —John Dewey (1933)

I started teaching in 1984. My journey of last thirty-four years of teaching has been very enriching. I learned that classroom pedagogy cannot be considered independently of the subjectivity of teacher, student and the curriculum. I reached this conclusion by learning to reflect on my experience in the classroom. As a young teacher, it took me some time to establish a connection with the students as my initial understanding was that I was an authority who had to 'teach.' In my first two years of teaching, I was really 'strict.' I used to enjoy being the one who could give direction. My fantasy was that working hard on my lectures and being prepared for the class meant that I would be in a position to answer the queries that students had and the class would be productive in thought. My classes were focused but I sensed that students were apprehensive about interacting with me.

I recall that once a student had to get a note from her parents as she could not submit her report. Not just her, the class as a collective was petrified of me. This is when I realized I needed to reflect on my perceptions of teaching. It encouraged me to begin a process of being engaged with systematic reflection on my teaching from students' learning. Through these reflections, I gradually learned what it meant to be a teacher. I got transformed from someone who essentially imagined herself in the classroom as an authority to a teacher who could be approached with questions, with experiences, and most importantly who wanted to establish a two-way connection.

Like most academic faculty, I was at many points overwhelmed during teaching. My punctuality created a further problem; the students were not excited to reach college for 8 am lectures. Their reluctance to show up for my class was the first thing I noticed. I had to rethink my approach and bring back my wit and humour. They needed to be punctual, but they also needed love and affection, and due excuses where warranted. This need for affection and openness materialized in their voices during tutorials. i.e. in small group interactions. They found it easier to communicate in smaller groups. They shared their thoughts, fantasies and worries, in short, their experiences.

Developing Pedagogy for Caring and Self-disclosure

It was at this juncture that I screened many movies but, let me underscore two movies that solidified my reflections i.e. *Dead Poets Society* and *To Sir, with Love*. These two movies made me confront an emerging question —what makes up the content and quality of my teaching. If a kind of know-how knowledge, aptitude and attitude is needed to be taught—what are they and how are they developed? And what do they imply for the person who enacts them? My questions were answered once caring and self-disclosure became part of my teaching process. It not only changed the quality of my lectures but also brought flexibility in transacting the curriculum.

I soon realized that my success as a teacher was contingent on the fact that first and foremost I needed to care about my students. Since then caring has been a scaffold for both cultivating and expecting my students to achieve their potential and self-fulfilment. Caring cannot happen without empathic listening. Mayeroff (1971) considers 'knowing, alternating rhythms, patience, honesty, trust, humility, hope, and courage as key aspects of a caring context' (p. 15). I, therefore, realized that teachers must consciously know their students and care for them in a responsive way. Kamala, for instance, failed in her second year of college. Despite warnings from teachers, Kamala was in a different world of dreams. As results were declared, the worst happened; she failed. When she came to the class with juniors, I could sense her anxiety, the loss of esteem and the onset of depression. I too was confused but was reflecting on what I could do to ease her transition in an old space with new unfamiliar classmates. When she was once absent from class, I decided to talk to the students about my own experience of failing in Class Two. I narrated how the sense of shame and my fellow students' laughter stayed with me as bitter memories throughout life. I explained what really bothered me was the indifferent role that my class teacher played at my dejection. I shared my vulnerability with the students. Bright as these junior students were, they realized that I wanted Kamala to experience warmth in the classroom which had friendly classmates. My interaction proved fruitful and Kamala blossomed in my class as an active participant. She now teaches at a reputed school.

Thus self-disclosure, a Rogerian contribution, is one starting point for such an investigation because self-revelation can set the affective and interpersonal tone of the classroom. Implicit in the claim 'how I teach is the message' is the recognition of teaching as a relational, social and public act. I think what is close to my heart is not my excellence as a teacher, but the words, 'AG ma'am just never gave up on me.' I learnt that listening to the surface text of what the student says and paying attention to the subtext of his/her subjectivity is critical. In my memory lane, I go back to Bartlett (1990) who used to point out that becoming a reflective teacher involves moving beyond a primary concern with instructional techniques and 'how to' questions and asking 'what' and 'why' questions that regard instructions and managerial techniques not as ends in themselves, but as part of broader educational purposes. Asking 'what and why' questions give us a certain power over our teaching. I can now claim that the degree of autonomy and responsibility I have in my teaching is determined by the level of control I can exercise on my subjectivity.

Setting the Space for Reflection

'A' lost her father at a young age to advanced stage cancer. At that time, she was working with me on a dissertation about cancer. However she did not share the news of her father's illness with me as he was diagnosed. As she completed the final year, she informed me of his death. She wanted me to come to the funeral. I remember her telling me how her family would not let her light the pyre as they believed in patriarchal Hindu traditions. I had taught her how these traditions were discriminatory towards women, and at that juncture where she demanded what was rightfully hers, I had to be there despite my fractured foot. She expected me to be there as the reinforcement of the theory she wanted to practise. In her agency being alive, my role was that I would back her in the need to relate to the dead father. This moment brought clarity in my mind about my bond with the students. Education is not just one little part of our existence as it is living a life. It is not just learning Wordsworth by heart; it is about feeling it and understanding why it is important. I feel that reflection is sometimes instinctive, and sometimes you need skills and rethinking of one's own actions, feelings and experiences. Effective Teaching demands a concept of reflection that is both deep and broad enough to encompass its ethical, subjective, political and emotional dimensions.

To some extent, reflection is hardwired into a teacher, but it is also a highly individual process, as unique as the student. In reflecting on the above kind of questions, we begin to exercise control and open up the possibility of transforming our everyday classroom life (Bartlett, 1990). Echoing in the movie, *To Sir, with Love*, a young Sydney Poitier throws the textbook into the trashcan of his raucous inner-city Liverpool classroom—a classic image in my mind and an unforgettable part of my memories about teachers and teaching. This inner dialogue and reflection taught me that a teacher cannot get caught up in forcing her students to finish their readings and assignments. Instead, the core of this stance is evolving a flexible approach to let the student share her questions, doubts and possible insights.

In order to avoid becoming the stuck and stubborn teacher, successful educators take time to reflect on their methods, their delivery, and the way they connect with their students. Also, there are so many students that you have to find a way out. As I gained experience, it became glaringly obvious what my students wanted was not just being taught a particular topic. Deep down, unconsciously, students wanted to be transformed so that their lives could become meaningful, happy and agentive.

Challenges in Praxis

As a first generational learner, it took me time to develop my capacity to immerse in my students' lives. Listening to them was critical. I wanted to be in tune with the student. But I struggled with practising listening, sometimes due to the environment of the class and sometimes with managing the course structures and curriculum specifics. There were students who would be absent and there were students who always distracted the class. My anger sometimes was drawn out of my struggle with how to develop a rubric. This is where I had to break away from old habits and let new ways of managing time and curriculum emerge. Teaching cannot just be instructional, it has to be a two-way process with the teacher and the students setting their own pace. Slowly, I absorbed the students' suggestions, in turn actively acknowledging their thoughts. I asked myself whether I could be both flexible and manage my impulsivity at the same time. It is only now I have learned that it is better to reflect before you speak as it is hard to fix a wrinkled heart.

Teaching means standing for something, for a specific idea of what constitutes an evolved life, a meaningful, and valuable life. Teaching implies taking a vantage point, choosing a particular ideology and engaging in its pursuit. This moral, subjective commitment, with its relationality and face-to-face engaging is an intrinsic part of teaching and therefore of teaching as a discipline. As Kelchtermans (2005), reminds us, teaching is fundamentally characterized and constituted by vulnerability. To my mind, vulnerability can be understood in two ways. Vulnerability is not so much to be understood as an emotional state or experience, though it triggers intense emotions. Here vulnerability is to be understood as an underlying characteristic of a teacher. Successful educators seek out a mentor for themselves. Reflective teachers can be vulnerable if they do not have support from both young and old colleagues. Mentors can be that voice that says, 'Yes you are moving towards earth-shattering reflections and sometimes you are talking trivia,' or 'No, you are somewhere else because...' and provide you with a different perspective. I recall Sammy, a student who experienced the difficult divorce of her parents. Rebel as she was, she troubled most of the teachers. When challenged, I realized that it stemmed from years of feeling uncared for at home. This need for love and care was voiced in her attempts of distracting the class. I have seen her combing hair, purposely getting the earphones on and questioning my understanding of family. I reflected on how I was cared for or not cared for by family as well as teachers. This insight of not accepting every family as a healthy family gave me a trajectory in which I could think and understand her and other students' subjectivity embroiled in too many complexities. This broadened my own horizon on how to provide care and support. Sometimes, I can justify my decisions explicitly with reference to a particular idea, but my judgement and decisions can always be challenged or questioned.

One of the most difficult aspects of teaching is the isolation it imposes on me. I spend most of my time in the classroom, with my students. There are very few opportunities to sit and observe, and learn from colleagues. Consequently, there is no possibility to consult with other colleagues, when you come across a difficult student or situation. As a young teacher, a pregnant student came to me for assistance for abortion. It shocked me to the core; I lost my sleep. Both her privacy and safety were critical. The ambivalence was whether I should simply fire her or empathize with her as a woman. A lecture on morality was the last thing on my mind. Teaching the curriculum was not my priority. This was really very discomforting. Yet, without these discomforting experiences, deep reflection—in which the content of one's personal interpretative framework is thoroughly challenged and questioned—will far less often be triggered. This moment took me to therapy in which my selfhood as a teacher could be moulded and reciprocity between the student and my own vulnerabilities becomes a reality.

At the heart and mind of my praxis is the student. Freire (1998) reminds us 'we must dare, in the full sense of the word, to speak of love without the fear of being ridiculous, mawkish, or unscientific, if not anti-scientific' (p. 3). This love that is there is not to parent them but to love them with 'constant intellectual rigor and the stimulation of epistemological curiosity, of the capacity to love, of creativity, of scientific competence and the rejection of scientific reductionism. The teaching task also requires the capacity to fight for freedom, without which the teaching task becomes meaningless' (p. 4).

Narratives of Experiential Learning

The concept of loving and caring for my students inspires me to be a more effective teacher. In order to be a better teacher, I must understand and deconstruct my own teaching through the reflexive process of teacher inquiry. What I have planned does not always happen but I remember Freire's (1987) statement that imagination and intuition 'mean to be strongly present, to have your feet firmly planted on the ground, in such a way that foreseeing the future becomes a normal thing. You know the present so well you can imagine a possible future of transformation' (p. 186). This transformation, therefore, is the key.

In my discovery of the student-teacher relationship, my students gradually seemed to realize how to love and care for everyone. They acquired maternal agency as they loved me through my tough times. I recall how some of my students were not happy with a young teacher who replaced me while I was not well. They wanted to be taught some difficult topics, so that they were comfortable going ahead to the difficult part of the semester. So I decided to teach while I was going through chemotherapy and radiation, they stood by me. Instead of my mother caring for me at home, I was cared for by thirty-two mothers (my students). Thus interdependence was another lesson that I learnt in evolving the teacher-student bond.

Whether it is the curriculum or relational issues, unless we confront the failure of the privileged and the powerful structures in a classroom, a fair humane academic world will not be possible. We need to find answers to more fundamental questions such as the meaning of humanity and at the same time safeguard against cynicism of teacher-student connection. While hope might be an accomplished liar, I believe that hope is all we have.

References

Dewey, John (1969-2008). *The Collected Works of John Dewey, 1882-1953*, 38 Vols., ed. Jo Ann Boydston (Carbondale, Illinois); 3rd electronic edition ed. Larry Hickman, accessible via http://www.nlx.com/.

Mayeroff, M. (1971). *On Caring*. New York: Harper and Row Publishers.

Bartlett, Leo (1990). Teacher development through reflective teaching. In J.C. Richards and D. Nunan (Eds.), *Second Language Teacher Education*. Cambridge: Cambridge University Press.

Kelchtermans, G. (2005). Teachers' emotions in educational reforms: Self-understanding, vulnerable commitment and micropolitical literacy. *Teaching and Teacher Education*, 21(8): 995-1006.

Freire, P. (1998). *Teachers as Cultural Workers: Letters to Those Who Dare Teach*. Boulder, CO: Westview Press.

Shor, I. and Freire, P. (1987). What is the 'dialogical method' of teaching? *Journal of Education*.

24
Reflections on Learning and Teaching

Vijaya Shankar Varma

It is claimed that to achieve excellence in any field of endeavour, one has to put in at least ten thousand hours of practice. A teacher in a college or university in India, according to UGC norms, has to teach for roughly two hundred days in a year. Assuming that she teaches one hour every day and spends about an hour on the average preparing a lesson, she would be putting in about four hundred hours of teaching related work every year and would require twenty-five years to fulfil such a norm. This is assuming that the teacher is able to maintain a steady level of commitment to excel at her work throughout these twenty-five years. Of course, she could do it faster if she were to commit more of her time to teaching her students.

I have personally spent almost thirty-five years teaching physics to postgraduate and undergraduate students. I did get better at my teaching with experience, at least initially, but I think my teaching skills followed a typical S-shaped trajectory, increasing rapidly in the beginning but then levelling off to a plateau from which they only declined slowly with increasing age.

There were a number of reasons why this was so. Physics in my early years of teaching attracted the brightest students who constantly challenged my understanding of what I was teaching so that I had to be constantly on my toes and be well prepared for my classes, often having to spend four hours in preparation for every hour I taught. When a lesson went well it was a source of great enjoyment. The difference in age between me, having just completed my PhD, and my students was a mere five to eight years. I was young enough in those days that those of my students, who were new to the University and did not know the teachers, often mistook me for a fellow student. Thus it was easy for both my students and me to relate to each other. I was also eager to prove myself at the beginning of my career, so I put in a lot of effort in my teaching. I was enthusiastic and also excited by the challenge of teaching new courses. Even though most subjects I taught, I had learnt when I was a student, it is one thing to learn a subject with a view to do well in examinations, and quite another to teach the same subject to a group of eager minds who are not averse to the prospect of tripping up their teacher whenever they sense any lack of clarity or understanding.

Teaching physics meant not only lecturing to students but also spending considerable time supervising their experimental work in the laboratory. Since the number of students enrolled in a course was usually very large, it was during laboratory supervision that I really got to know my students. Very often they would be performing experiments seriously for the first time in their lives, given the lack of laboratory facilities in most schools in India and reflective of the little importance, given to experimentation in science teaching in our schools. This meant that many students really needed help in performing their experiments seriously and honestly. This was compounded by the lack of maintenance of the laboratory equipment, which were often old-fashioned and not in good condition. So when things went wrong or the results of the experiments were not what they were expected to be, there was strong pressure on the students to 'cook' their results instead of trying to find out what had gone wrong by repeating their work and trying to improve the accuracy of their observations. This was a major challenge to the teachers because it could not be done sitting at their desks and speculating on all the things that could have gone wrong or by preaching the need for accurate experimentation, good practice and the virtues of careful and systematic work.

If you really wanted to help your students you had to go to their workbenches, observe carefully how they were performing their experiment and show them exactly what they were doing wrong. If you did this supervision honestly and diligently and did not try to fob them off with some obscure reason why they were not getting the expected results, you could earn their respect and develop bonds that extended beyond the confines of the classrooms and laboratories and in the process you sometimes even made lifelong friends.

There were other ways you bonded with your students. When you are not much older than them you can join them in their extracurricular activities, in debates and quizzes, engage in sports with them, help them with their ideas and with the exhibitions that they put up and guide them in their project work. You have to be careful not to be condescending in your attitude, to be genuinely respectful of their opinions and treat them as autonomous beings. All this comes easily when you are young, but as you grow older, even though you gain experience and maybe even get wiser, the difference between your age and the age of the students you teach, keeps increasing and it progressively becomes more and more difficult to keep doing what you had been doing when you were younger and more energetic. Your family responsibilities increase; you get caught up in more and more administrative work and do not realize that over time the attitudes of your students are no longer what you had grown accustomed to. I also found that the motivation levels of my students kept dropping as the years went by; many of them no longer found learning basic physics to be attractive. Market forces encouraged increasing parental pressure on students to enroll in what were considered to be more attractive courses with promises of higher salaries and more comfortable lives. As the quality of the intake of students in physics declined, the difficulties and effort required to teach them the existing syllabus increased correspondingly. Whereas earlier the majority of the students had been eager to learn the intricacies and the nuances of the subject, it slowly came to pass that no more than a tenth of the students were interested in learning anything at all. They had enrolled in physics because they could not get admission in the courses they really wanted and being at a university was in any case better than wandering around doing nothing. There was always the possibility that they could pick up a degree on the way, a certificate that did not necessarily give them a job but without which they had no hope of getting one. Our department had slowly been transformed into a crèche for grown-up children, keeping them off the streets and out of trouble. The syllabus, which had been designed for students with an altogether different level of ability and commitment, became impossible to teach and the motivation levels all-around, students and teachers included, plummeted through the floor.

A couple of comments are in order. Teaching a class of bright young students was very enjoyable but also a stressful experience for me; the stress arose from the amount of preparation that I found I had to do as well as from the anxiety to teach them well. My other comment is based on the experience of enrolling in a course of Hungarian halfway through my career as a teacher. I found I had forgotten the struggle involved in learning a new subject and it made me realize the difficulties my own students must have faced in trying to understand what I was teaching. I found it to be a great learning experience and it provided me many useful insights into the teaching-learning process. I would strongly recommend that every teacher after teaching for a number of years should sign up for a new course of study, not only to learn something new but also to be reminded of the problems students face in learning.

Fortunately for me, the disillusionment with trying to teach reluctant students happened towards the time of my retirement from the university. I have often wondered since, whether I could I have done anything to change the situation, particularly about motivating the majority of my students to take more interest in what I was teaching. Even though after retirement, I have not been called upon to teach, other than one course on the philosophy and methods of science, my association with students and higher education has fortunately continued with engagement in planning and administration. Having had time to reflect on the issue, I believe one way we could increase the motivation levels of students, in the current scenario of falling interest in academics in general, is by looking into our traditions of teaching and learning. This is not a call for the kind of revival of interest in our heritage that our politicians are promoting these days, by for example claiming that the *brahmāstra* of the *Mahābhārat* were atomic weapons or that Rāma's arrows were nothing other than ballistic missiles. I am not advocating a return to our myths and spiritual heritage but to our rational, sceptical, epistemic traditions in which schools of philosophy, both *nāstika* and *āstika,* even when wedded to contending metaphysical and ontological positions, vied and debated with each other for centuries on the nature of existence and what constituted reality. Their shared central concern was the alleviation of human suffering and they all agreed, rightly or wrongly, that the root cause of all human suffering was ignorance. Thus the quest for knowledge became a matter of the highest importance to all philosophical schools and they, through their debates and discussions, developed a theory of knowledge that is a counterpoint to the theory of knowledge in the western tradition. *Pramāṇa* theory, which was developed by these schools through constant debate and discussion, deals with the nature and source of knowledge as well as the different valid ways of knowing. Etymologically, the root of the word is *'mā'* which means to measure. So *pramāṇa* is that by which something is measured and therefore an instrument for acquiring knowledge that is reliable and in principle also true. A *pramāṇa* is therefore both an authoritative process for acquiring knowledge, and also a means of ensuring that the knowledge so acquired is valid. It deals not only with the reasons why any piece of knowledge is to be considered justified from an epistemic point of view but also with the reasons for the validity of such justification. Over time, different schools of thought developed different notions on what these valid ways of knowing are.

Although the primary process of acquiring valid knowledge that was acceptable to all schools of thought was sensory perception (*pratyaksa*), the number and different kinds of *pramāṇas* was a contentious issue among the different schools. The *Cārvāka* accepted only sense perception and none other as a source of reliable knowledge. The Buddhist accepted both perception and inference (*anumāna*). The Sānkhya accepted perception, inference and testimony (*śabda*); the Nyāya accepted perception, inference, testimony and comparison (*upamāna*); the Pūrva Mīmānsā accepted perception, inference, testimony, comparison and presumption (*arthāpatti*); while the Advaita Vedānta accepted perception, inference, testimony, comparison, presumption and non-cognition (*anuplabdhi*) as valid *pramāṇas*. These different views on what constitutes a *pramāṇa* came to determine the ontologies and the metaphysics of the different schools of Indian philosophy.

The reason for bringing this up in this essay is that ways of teaching cannot be divorced from ways of knowing and that the study of our traditional ways of knowledge could both help us become better teachers and at the same time provide clues to ways in which one could revive the interest of our students in academic pursuits, so that they become more efficient learners and better-equipped to find solutions to the problems in their academic lives. While we try and incorporate in our pedagogy an alternative to the dominant Western model, an alternative to which our students may be more receptive, we should also be aware of and try to emulate our old traditions of rational debate and the plurality of the approaches of the different schools of Indian philosophy.

That said, we must not forget that many of the problems we encounter as teachers at the tertiary level often have their roots in how education is organized in our schools. The problems are many and many solutions can and have been proposed. However, one potential cause that seems to have been ignored in the main is that we have a fractured view of our education system. We lack an overall integrated vision—the organisation of higher education is seen as separate from and largely independent of the organisation of school education. There is only marginal and perfunctory participation by a few chosen teachers from tertiary education in the framing of school syllabi and a similarly casual participation of schoolteachers in the writing of school textbooks. Other than that, the landscape of mutual participation and engagement in school and university education is a barren and arid desert. A greening of this desert would require a major revision of the role that the universities see for themselves in school education and the realization that such revision does not have to wait for a change in government policy.

25

Empathy as Meandering

Recalling Some Moments from a Life Led with Students

Rachana Johri

In writing this piece on empathetic and reflective pedagogy, I find myself caught up in reminiscences of a long journey that is still ongoing. It is not easy to sieve through these memories, particularly as I grapple with my present location in a more difficult world that promises much, yet seems to produce new difficulties. This is not a theorized piece of writing. Rather it is my first attempt to go through a process that started in 1985 and continues into the present, a process dedicated in a large measure to my attempt to be a 'good' teacher. It is difficult for me to reflect upon my experiences of teaching without turning towards my own difficulties as a student. As a child, I was painfully shy. I am told I cried 'buckets full of tears' when my parents dropped me off at school. As I grew up, I developed my own combination of vulnerabilities and resources. I was a good student. Learning came easily to me. I had good friends and spoke easily in class. Yet, these strengths remained only as long as I was in a familiar or a comfortable setting. In anything less familiar, I froze, experiencing what I would now call, performance anxiety. My own experience of shyness has mediated my relationship with teaching. The sight of many unfamiliar faces when I first enter a classroom remains a daunting one for me. In known and unknown ways, each batch I teach is a new negotiation with diversity, an attempt at creating an environment where learning can take place without injury.

I decided to study Psychology because it occupied a space amongst my favourite subjects at school: biology, history and literature. I had always enjoyed learning and psychology taught me about multiple facets of human experience. The years doing my Masters and MPhil brought me closer to other social sciences. These furthered an engagement with three spheres of psychology—the experience of mental illness, the lives of women and the processes of child-development. I worked with the mentally ill and tried out feminist psychotherapy with women who came to me to discuss their troubles. These were the sources of reflexivity that formed the subtexts as I taught my favourite domains, Child Development, Counselling and Systems of Psychology at Lady Shri Ram College (LSR) for Women (University of Delhi), moving to Ambedkar University Delhi (AUD) only in 2011, more than 25 years after I began. The context in which I came to join AUD in 2011 was radically different. We were given complete freedom to design courses. In LSR, feminism could at best permeate my classes, seeping in through a gentle critique of mainstream psychology. I knew some of the young women sitting in the classroom 'got it', but it was never my primary target to create ideological subjects. Today when I reflect upon this, there is nostalgia for the past, an uncanny sense that the structured spaces of academic autonomy I have here are not always greater than the resisting space within which I taught at LSR, but that is perhaps another story.

Teaching Undergraduate Psychology

Like others of my time, I taught everything that was expected of me. We did not design our own courses then and one part of the exercise of teaching was to ensure that the largest numbers did well in a one-time examination they would be asked to write. The question paper set by some unknown examiner would often be mundane; the primary skill required was to produce as fast as possible the answers that would get them the highest marks. When I think back to the years of teaching, I wonder if I was conscious of the requirements of empathy or transformation? My first concern was that students were not enjoying the learning process. The task before me was to create a desire for learning in students. The challenge was to make everything interesting and relevant to their stage of life. I applied whatever I had understood from my education: the role of families and schools in undermining the value of education particularly for women. I also applied the belief I took from Carl Rogers (1961) that unconditional acceptance and empathy can open up the growth potential of people and the spirit contained in Erik Erikson's thoughts on youth as a stage of identity crisis with an inherent potential for transformation (Schlein, 1995). My first assumption was that most students had not experienced the environment that facilitated an interest in knowledge. Many students hated the classroom, coming to it only because a Bachelor's degree was deemed to be a requirement to complete their qualifications for adulthood, even if that meant getting married to the man, the family chose for them. The only transformation I was working on was to make learning joyful. So classes were about examples from life regardless of whether we were discussing intelligence testing or Freud.

Despite my orientation towards qualitative and interpretive psychologies, I taught positivist aspects of psychology long after I had lost commitment to them. In fact, the structures within which I worked did not allow me to forget mainstream psychology. I looked instead for ways to understand the diverse directions the discipline had taken. Why did psychology take such a predominantly Behaviouristic turn in 1914 that continued till the 1960s ? What is the desire to control and predict behaviour? When do we like to be controlled and predictable? Teaching Behaviourism lovingly, was like an act of reclaiming disowned selves. There was a time when I was fascinated by B.F. Skinner, the American behavioural psychologist. Owning up these old forgotten selves served several purposes. At one level, it allowed me to develop an understanding of the historical and political processes involved in the emergence of Behaviourism. I tried to bring the question of the location of forms of understanding in larger contexts to the students. At the same time, I attempted a 'clinical study' of Behaviourism and later of other forms of psychology. To do this, I tried to imagine the pursuit itself, rendering it as full of meaning for my students as it was possible for me to do. It was only after the meaning had been established that the critique would begin. I believe the method worked. Not only did I communicate the various perspectives of the discipline to the class, I also enabled them to find a home somewhere amongst them. And because every aspect was rendered meaningful and yet incomplete, students felt at ease even when they knew that what they loved was not my way of looking at the world. Sometimes they would say to me outside the classroom, 'you know I like the clarity of Behaviourism. I like Scientific Psychology'. The fact that this conversation was possible was my success.

Yet, I was not a Behaviourist at all. I found myself resonating with the Interpretive Psychologies of Psychoanalysis, Humanism and Existentialism. I was particularly drawn to theorists who wrote about the lives of children and the distressed from a psychosocial perspective. Erik Erikson (1995) had spoken of the significance of identity crisis and moratorium. For me, this provided a framework through which to approach my students as much as the question of pedagogy. At the same time, I saw myself as a feminist and teaching provided some space to introduce questions of power in the construction of identities.

Diversity in the Classroom

In the initial years I was confused. Sitting in the class before me were thirty-five faces with distinct profiles. In those days we did not think about differences in the elaborate manner that we do now. Although diversity within campuses has probably increased, University of Delhi always drew students from across India and each one of them had come with their own expectations of college life. Amongst those I faced were bright young girls willing to question the world, others who had struggled for the right to some education and wanted a first division, those completely committed to sports and finally those for whom being in college was the most boring aspect of their life. The latter came to class dressed for a party, distracted by the imagination of their boyfriends outside, fidgeting and restless, waiting to run away. The official task assigned to me was to convert them all into scholars with a passionate desire to understand the workings of the world, spend most hours of their lives reading and writing and experiencing the depression of knowing that the world was an unfair place. If this was not sufficiently taxing for them, I added to it by the expectation that they would all idealize a few of the identity options available to them. To make me happy, students would need to value either the space of academics or the task of working with the distressed.

I cannot deny these were my ideals, but I was faced with a dilemma. Whom should I be teaching? And how? The answers to these questions are complex and remain uncertain. However, over the years, I found myself trying to be a teacher who could see meaning in the diverse aspirations with which students came to college.

Teaching/Reaching the Group

I did enjoy teaching and was grateful that I had the opportunity to work in a college where classes took place regularly and students had greater facility of language than in similar spaces. I suppose my first step was always to communicate my love for the discipline to them. Mostly, this worked but I remember one afternoon, trying to teach about the nature of abnormality and the presence of the abnormal in each of us. 'Didn't they sometimes feel they had symptoms?', I asked and was astounded to hear them respond in the negative. 'They'd never felt anxious or depressed'? 'Not really'. It was not easy to teach a batch such as this one for the entire year and it was traumatic to realize that it was possible for young people to disown distress.

I begin here, not because it was my dominant experience. Most of my years of teaching were joyous ones, despite mass bunks and missed assignments. The question before me was whether I could recognize my redundancy in certain contexts. How could I do so without experiencing rage and victimizing students? My discipline has taught me that there are reasons why people choose to think in particular ways. I am only one of the persons they meet in their lives. Many are forced by parents and the social norms around them to come for undergraduate education. Others are struggling because they are seen as complete failures because they chose psychology. The question of empathetic pedagogy includes the question of resistance. What if the students are deeply resistant to my theorization of the subjective? Over the years, I became more patient and more passionate, more humorous and more concerned, trying to shape but also give space. Knowing the discipline well was significant to giving students a sense of trust but recognizing that it did not have the same place in each trajectory that it did in mine was equally significant.

I remember an attempt at a small group discussion when I asked the students what they enjoyed reading. It used to be Sydney Sheldon. It is Chetan Bhagat now, I suspect. I was quite astounded when I heard one of them cheerfully tell me that the only reading she ever did was page three of Delhi Times. I was somewhat horrified but took it in my stride. There was no point in advising her as I routinely did with other students that they look for better newspapers and read the editorial pages. I just laughed at it along with her. A few years ago in a chance encounter, I met a man on a train travelling from Lucknow to Delhi. For the longest part of the journey, he was on the mobile phone discussing details of business transactions. Finally, when all that was over, he asked me a few questions which led me to mention my profession. Excitedly, he wondered if I might have taught his daughter. To my surprise he was the father of the page three kid. He quickly dialled her on the phone and I found myself chatting with my once student. I have wondered for very long why I remember this student so well. She was perhaps an other to me, completely outside my worldview but full of cheer and good humour. I often wonder what such students remember of the higher education they received, but it is difficult to imagine that it made no impression upon them.

I suppose the fact that I loved the profession helped. Teaching meant reaching every student at some level. Inside the class, I forgot the world outside specially if I was teaching a course I valued. I recall seeing the students' eyes gleam when they understood something for the first time. It was a heady experience. The most important consideration was to try and let students ask questions. Yet there was no recipe for success. I was accused by one I remember clearly who said "you have your favourites. You prefer the ones who speak good English. You like Dilliwalis." She was probably correct. In the years after she left, I became more attuned to the needs of young women who had migrated to Delhi for undergraduate education and several remain friends years after college was over.

Negotiating Students' Conflicts

One narrative I heard frequently concerned the deeply confusing experience of college. The social sciences revealed a world that was extremely different from the ideology of the families they came from. They could not see how to bring them together. I could see their distress but could not answer their questions. Mostly I asked if life could be entirely without distress? Sometimes I suggested that they give themselves time. Perhaps answers would come slowly. One thing I knew was that biographies were important. Erikson helped to think through the problem. Each student would have to find their own answer, one that was possible for her to live with. One of the issues I faced almost every year concerned conflict between parents and children. In the initial years, I expected students to find the courage to fight against their parents. Over the years, my position changed. I began to suggest that students give time to parents, that parents often experience anxiety about the well-being of their children and believe that it is their responsibility to prevent any damage to them. I suggested that the students find intermediate goals that would defer the moment of confrontation, to recognize that families too feel powerless. Parents needed the certainty that their 'children' had become 'responsible'. Once they acquired that confidence they too would be less afraid.

I still remember Sadhna, one of the brightest students I had ever taught telling me she wanted to do her Master's degree abroad and that she had no choice but to get married after the BA course was over. She seemed certain that the path to education was now over for her. It seemed a terrible waste of her potential to me and I asked her to speak at least once to her father. Reluctantly, she asked and was taken aback when he negotiated to allow her to go abroad for her Master's. I met Sadhna several times in the ensuing years. She had developed a passionate involvement in the field of education, her then existence a far cry from the world her parents had initially planned for her.

I remember too, Radhika looking very disturbed, unable to concentrate. She was interested in art but was pursuing psychology for a degree. She did not like psychology nor was she able to cope with the pressure of doing both. Such encounters were more difficult for me than those with the non-conformist students and those like Sadhna who wanted more education. However, I could see her interest and encouraged her to do psychology for a while longer, giving it some time. She could always return to art later and give up psychology. To my surprise psychology became an abiding interest for her. She went on to complete her PhD and is now a practising psychologist.

Despite my love for it, I had my own dissatisfactions with my discipline. Many students talked of their disappointment with mainstream psychology. Amongst my closest students, several have gone on to study sociology, literature and even history and law. There are others doing excellent work in NGOs and political spaces. When Kavita, brilliant, silent and thoughtful told me years ago that she wanted to be a Civil Servant, my heart sank. I do not remember if I dissuaded her. We just read interesting texts, and had wide-ranging discussions in tutorials. The students simply gave us the chance to bring these to them and something changed. I feel I contributed something to them. On reflection, a part of it was acceptance. It was the refusal to become a parental figure who knew what was best for them. Kavita and others have achieved a degree of commitment to the marginal in India that far exceeds my own. Yet their being in touch assures me and gives me the confidence to continue to teach despite the changing times.

Love, Marriage and Motherhood

The question of love and marriage was a recurrent theme in students' lives. I found myself occupying a paradoxical position. I was already married by the time I started work and a mother six years later. Yet I discussed these critically in the class and fostered an ideology of individuation and choice. It was not surprising then that I heard many stories of secret relationships and the fear of parental disapproval. I encouraged students to pursue the relationships of their choice, seeing it as a right that parents could not bring themselves to impinge upon. However I also tried to explore the nature of the relationship. What was it that the young woman before me was calling love? Were parents being simply casteist or generally conservative or did they sense that their daughter was not yet ready for the choice she seemed to be making? In class, we discussed identity crisis as much as masochism in love. It is hard for someone as unromantic as me to say this, but love did turn out to conquer all, at least in some of the lives I had listened to.

We were talking about faith one day in a tutorial class. Deeksha started to speak of the peace she experienced when she went to listen to the sermons of one of the women in her hometown. As we listened to her the narrative turned to the sudden death of Deeksha's sister. I was stunned. I had already grown to admire this girl for the questions she asked and the answers she wrote. But I had no idea of the trauma she had experienced. I hoped that she would continue to study psychology. AUD was already in existence by that time but I suppressed my disappointment when I heard that Deeksha was pursuing her Master's from another university outside Delhi. Once there, Deeksha started calling frantically in distress. She missed the world she had left, and missed the reflective openness of the classes. Although the course she had chosen required the cultivation of empathy, she could not see it amidst her faculty there. I was worried. I could see a breakdown coming and it did. Deeksha would call me and I would give her as much time as possible. Then she met a boy and fell in love. I was pleased but the stories she told me were scary too. Meanwhile there was the question of community. Would her family accept him? I did not know and when she did speak to them they were adamant in their opposition. However Deeksha's sorrows were not over. Her father was getting progressively unwell. One day I received a call from her.'Something terrible has happened', she said. I knew from her voice that something grave had taken place but even i could not believe it when she told me her younger sister had died in an accident. I was silent. I knew Deeksha would now be the only child, grieving for her siblings, needing to support her parents and without the presence of her friend. Although she did complete her degree, Deeksha had to return home after that. Doubly insecure now, her parents were desperate that she marry a man of their choice. Deeksha was terribly distressed but insisted she could only marry her friend at the university. I remember my confusion. Would he really be there for her? She had already given up on career opportunities to be with her parents. I understood this was essential for her well-being. Yet, I knew she needed to resist their pressure regarding marriage and I supported her decision to refuse the offers that came her way. Ultimately, Deeksha got married to her friend. Perhaps she will return to her career someday, and perhaps she will find an alternative passion.

Although Deeksha's family critiqued her choice of partner, I do not recollect any reference to violence. And while I did myself foreground the need to understand parental anxiety earlier in this writing, resistance is important when parents become violent towards their daughters. Partners too are often physically and sexually abusive. These are the moments I have found the hardest to negotiate. Some years ago, a young woman, Madhavi, asked me if she could speak to me. She came from a conservative but rich family but was exceedingly depressed. As I listened to her, I learnt that she had been 'in love' with a boy for several years. She had showered him with gifts, creating elaborate stories to ward off her father who monitored every payment she made from her credit card. Some time back the boy asked her to have sex with him since they had been together for a while. She agreed, only to find that the relationship had become public by the next day. She was depressed and hated herself. Worse, her father had smelt a rat and was becoming increasingly angry with her. He insisted that she left Delhi and studied elsewhere. In the short time I met Madhavi I tried to contain her shame and self-hate. Was she not right in wanting to sleep with the man she had been with for so long? Was he not the one who was hateful? I tried reaching out to her after she left but could not trace her. Madhavi was young but it has been difficult for many of our students to walk out of violent relationships even when they are more resourceful. It is here that I find myself swinging between frustration and compassion, remaining connected to the dependent vulnerable self that cannot quite go it alone, yet despairing that there may be no end to the story. Still, on reflection, when small autonomies are gained, work becomes better and finally the courage might be found to make the exit.

On another note, consider a married student Suman who got unexpectedly pregnant. The student was still in college and asked me, 'What shall I do?' I was quiet. 'The baby will come in the middle of the year. It will be very difficult to complete the semester'. I asked in turn, what did she want? She seemed to want the baby, as the pregnancy had happened. Fine, I said.' Ho jayega'. And she did manage, despite many difficulties. One day, after the baby was born, I was teaching infant attachment. Babies love their caretakers and not necessarily the natural mother. Poignantly she shared, "you know I think my baby loves his grandmother more than me." It was probably true. Babies are quite democratic about love but I knew how much this could hurt the mother. I agreed with her. The infant would 'fall in love' with his/her primary caretaker, not the biological mother. However, that did not mean that he would not love her too. The love might be different and weaker initially but would soon assume a quality of its own. Being a good mother in such a situation required her to contain the feelings of sorrow, guilt and envy she must have felt even though they were perfectly understandable. I told her about the advantages of multiple mothering from the child's perspective. It was only a matter of months before the separation would be over and she would return to the everyday care of her child.

On Deadlines and Emotional Crises

Deadlines of writing create their own emotional crises particularly in the age of subjectivity. Recognizing the connection of thoughts to personal histories is empowering although it is in no way the only route to questions. Yet, it also creates difficulties in completing the work in hand. Each year, as we supervise students there are some who seem unable to manage. Quite often the difficulty is not of intellect, and not even of writing. They are excellent performers but find it difficult to theorize around an area that has evocative significance for them. The clarity of deadlines, the messiness of psychic processes and the panic associated with voicing thoughts in one's own name create a potent compound for creating states of breakdowns. As a supervisor too, one has several tasks here. The first two are those deemed to be the designated role of the supervisor. He/ she should enable students to receive their degrees and create for themselves the freedom to explore new opportunities and create a piece of work that meets acceptable standards.

Erikson would call these aspects of competence that a student acquires from an educational system. This competence could also be thought of as the tools through which to negotiate the world of work. But Erikson also reminds us of the emergence of crises, particularly at times when young people are caught between the moralities of families and of the new worlds that academics open out to them. He reminds us that young people need mentoring persons who will oversee the passage of the crisis without the experience of too many deadlines. It is as if they need to sharpen their tools without feeling that they will mutilate themselves or cause significant hurt to others in their lives.

This is a crisis I have lived through several times with my students. It has been particularly difficult for me because in my own life I rarely miss deadlines. Yet I sometimes feel that my own superego has been too harsh. While I come across as competent enough, my work has lacked the spark I believe some of my students have. My own work as a mentor/supervisor has been to create some ease for students in panic. This has meant emphasizing deadlines in the first instance but equally recognizing sources of distress that may act as temporarily disabling. In such moments, it is the time period available that needs to be made flexible. Of course time is flexible. The dissertation can be submitted later, and the entire degree can be completed in three years too. As I have sat with students and shared with them that I would not be compromised, nor experience shame by their delays, I have, I believe, taken away one source of stress from the students' experienced states. Over the years, most have submitted their work on schedule but there have been a few instances when time was needed and seeking the longer time frame has allowed them to find a voice, evidenced in their later choice of careers.

And a Horrible Failure

I cannot end this writing without a brief mention of a failure that haunts me. I will not write of it in any detail except to acknowledge that Rati, who cried with me, fought hard, loved too much and could not love enough, taught me the limits of my capabilities. With Rati, I learnt that an intellectual facade and brilliant performances may sometimes mask deep insecurities. She taught me to teach carefully, to set limits to being provocative, to watch carefully the multiplicity inside the classroom, and to not only teach the expressive but also transpose to worry about damage to the vulnerable self. Now when sharing is required I speak of myself rather than ask for disclosures. I have, I admit, been somewhat scarred.

This writing and the years have healed my scars somewhat but I remain concerned about the role of higher education in students' lives. What do we do when we attempt to transform? What is transformation without empathetic care? What is a safe classroom? I still struggle with these questions but feel even more worried when I look at the changing notions of time and performance in the contemporary culture. Will we retain the space for empathy in a system that is becoming increasingly rigid in its expectations of attendance and other formalities? How can I bring my tacit expectations of individuation, of feminist transformation to a class that is diversely constituted through its students and fixed by the nature of course work. How can we teach a wider variety of courses when the resources for hiring additional faculty are limited?

I have tended to believe students when they speak of confusion and distress. I prefer to give them time to sort themselves out. I do not hate incomplete work, nor poor performance although I will not deny the sheer pleasure of reading a brilliant piece of writing. Creating a space of empathetic pedagogy requires the capacity to care for multiple others. It is labour that consumes us even as we are enriched by it. As we move into an increasingly global world, a world in which we too are measured in terms of API points, I am not worried that our standards will fall. Indeed our students today receive better education than any of us did. Yet, as the structure of education changes, I worry that our own imaginations of ourselves will become increasingly steered by productivity. Will this leave the space for empathetic pedagogy?

(All the names mentioned in the text are fictitious).

References

Rogers, C. (1961). *On Becoming a Person: A Therapist's View of Psychotherapy.* New York: Houghton Mifflin Company.

Schlein, S. (Ed.) (1995). *Erik H. Erikson: A Way of Looking at Things. Selected Papers.* New York: WW Norton and Company.

26

Reminiscences and Explorations of a Teacher in Becoming

Honey Oberoi Vahali

Teaching, like loving and living, is an ongoing process. As the strings of the harp meet the finger and music flows through their momentary contact, teachers and students touch each other to be unmade and made anew. This mutuality casts its deep imprints on our being. Our students break and recreate us; we make and remake them. Teaching is an ethical, political and spiritual journey. It is precious for precisely the reason that it never converts us into a finished product. We are forever in the flow of becoming.

A long time back, Rabindranath Tagore said, a lamp has to burn itself in order to ignite the flame of another lamp. A teacher knows that sooner than later her students, and especially the ones closest to her, will challenge her ideas, confront her truths and eventually go beyond them. It is her ethic to lovingly survive the process of being temporarily destroyed and questioned. Like in many other intimate relationships, love and violence intrinsically coexist in the teaching-learning situation. However, knowing this intellectually and going through the same at the experiential level are two altogether different processes. In a sense, this write-up is also about a teacher's journey though such transitions.

A Reverie

Often when I have asked myself what it means to be a teacher, an image has returned to me. I see a landscape, perhaps a garden, perhaps an open piece of land, strewn with invisible but nevertheless living seeds that sprout here and there into tiny leaves and grass, little shrubs, moderate-size plants and also magnificently looming trees. This non-homogenized garden grows at its own pace, facilitated as it is by the life-imparting sources of nature within whose lap it resides. The forms of energy that develop roots within this piece of earth have an intimate relationship with the seeds from which they spring forth, as also with the provisions of care and facilitating conditions of nature that make it possible for each of them to reach their potential flowering.

Our classrooms too are like this piece of earth. Students come to us with varying potentials—the inlaid promise in each one of them that seeks fruition and life. They come from different families, class backgrounds, economic possibilities, social, gender and cultural set-ups and personal life situations. For some, generations behind them have enjoyed reading, writing and thinking. Education for this set of students is a natural path and a taken-for-granted reality. Others come from familial contexts where no one has ever reached a college or seen what a university is really like. For them, the idea of modern education is an unfamiliar one. Some take to classroom discourses like fish to water. Others begin to engage with modern educational concepts and thoughts only after struggling through many taken-for-granted steps. For still others access to English language is a major hurdle to be overcome.

The fact that our students have reached so far, invokes the promise to take them through a journey. In my imaginative reverie, a teacher has to become an organic gardener who does some trimming but who is in general comfortable with growth amidst non-uniformity and wilderness. The task of this gardener is a paradoxical one. Having a loose design in mind, the gardener has to be at ease with plants growing out of harmony, with the hedges not being well-trimmed, nor all the flowers blooming at the expected time. If the gardener is passionate about a 'perfect and well-kept uniform garden', she will uproot and kill many small plants. She will end up cutting the unequal edges in an attempt to trim them to size. In doing so, she is likely to destroy many seeds that do not fit the uniform design of his choice.

As an organic gardener, our role is like that of an 'ordinarily devoted mother'. As the British psychoanalyst, D.W. Winnicott said, 'we do not have to be exceptional human beings to be good enough mothers' (1967). Instead a good enough mother is able to feel the specific needs of her child or each of her children even though she inevitably fails in her provision of care every now and then. Ask a mother and she will tell you how at times she can only find contentment with failing better instead of perfectly rising to the demands of the situation. In other moments, in spite of feeling frustrated, she is able to return with renewed love and care for her children. In this oscillating and non-linear process of attunement and misattunement, she may intuitively learn to be a different mother to each of her children—adjusting herself in resonance with their particular temperaments. Similarly as teachers and facilitators, we would do well to see the classroom as a distinctive space and know that there is no one measure, nor one uniform pace for the growth of the entire class.

The translation of the above into an ethic of practice in my teaching has implied my need to acknowledge the differential paces of my students' growth. This also meant that I had to be in touch with a variety of their human qualities and attributes, strengths and promises. Gradually it became important to cherish the idea that my job was to affirm the best in each student, rather than search for the best student. In my search for the best in each student, I had to open up myself to appreciate the beauty in what each one of them was capable of. With the passage of time, I noticed this spontaneous inclination took me towards gently attending to the distinctive and particular trajectories of different students' growth.

A further learning awaited me here. Academic climate in a university can sometimes be very violent. In more than any other space, it is in the intellectual spaces that the 'sovereign power' of critique is rationalized. In the process, we often forget to dwell on the means and ethical imperatives of this process. Critique can easily convert itself into violent criticism and university spaces can continue to justify it in the name of advancement of knowledge. The power hidden in the process can so easily be ignored. To me this seemed counterproductive to the task of nurturing young minds. I thought that as a teacher I had tremendous power to ruthlessly uproot or gently transform the learners in my class. I did not want to uproot them. I wanted to foster growth by according significance to their thoughts, whatever they were and thus taking them through a facilitative process. I have held this as a precious value in my mind for a time much longer than since I have been able to express it in words. I am mindful, this is a tall order for any teacher to put into practice; I do not know if I have succeeded in this direction. However I consider it as an important way of subverting the individualistic, alienating and competitive ethos of the historical times of which we all, including our educational systems, are a collective part of.

From Then to Now

If I were to describe in words, I think I practise a form of critical and experientially-oriented education which is founded on the principles of empathy and care, and it is also a vision of relating to others in a non-consumerist manner. My field of teaching is primarily psychotherapy and like most fields of practice in medicine and higher education, today it is likely to be endangered by burgeoning market forces that can easily convert it into a consumable commodity. The threat of commercialization is real. Therefore there is a self-conscious stress in my teaching to envision the practice of psychotherapy as a non-commercial process. I also focus on the experiences and needs of those existing on socio-economic margins. Further,

I encourage self-reflexive thinking in students around how notions of achievement in life and the monetization of the mind go hand in hand in the modern day capitalist cultures. This helps in releasing an understanding of care which is relatively freer from the dominant hegemonies of our times. By introducing ripples of disquiet and by questioning the silent acceptance of normalizing discourses, a critical angle is introduced in the classroom which is then taken ahead through an experiential process.

When I was a younger teacher, I rigorously prepared for classes. I was eager to take my students through concepts, theories and ideas and completing the syllabus. I was complimented by students for my ability to clearly communicate difficult ideas. However even then, I considered the relational dimensions in the student-teacher bond to be of immense value. Over the years, I have moved on to becoming more of a facilitator who first encourages waves of experiential sharing in the classroom and later balances the same with theoretical inputs, research in the tradition as well as contributions from interdisciplinary currents.

As I look back, I realize, in my initial years I invoked theory and concepts in the classroom with a hope that they would help students connect to real life contexts. With time and experience, I have arrived at a sense of greater ease. Now I am more intimately in touch with the realm of knowledge (both in my students and myself) which is born from and which pulsates with the pressing questions, dilemmas and strivings of our everyday life. This is contextual and rooted in the vicissitudes of human subjectivity and life history. Therefore the modes of teaching I employ serve to bridge the gap between classroom discourses and actualities of lived life. They allow for a host of expressions in the classroom. These forms of engagement provide me with an opportunity to join access to education with the inclusion of divergent voices, especially the hitherto marginalized ones. They also impart a greater mutuality to our interactions. None of us is an expert here. We are cotravellers. In the experiential realm, at times I may have something worthwhile to share, and at other times; the students expand the horizon of my knowledge, as also the consciousness of the group as a whole.

I often shift gears in my role as a facilitator. In almost all instances, I find myself encouraging the class to develop a critical intellectual mindset and to rethink the complacency of the normalizing discourses. Simultaneously we reach questions which help us to reflect on structural power and its impact, especially on neglected lives. At other times, we try to explore possible connections of the above with pressing existential dilemmas in students' personal lives. Guided by a psychoanalytic framework which values the wisdom and silent healing strength of the unconscious, teaching becomes a process of initiating students into the joyful discovery of mystery, the playful spirit of surprise and the deepening which comes by keeping alive an axis wherein the 'inside' and the 'outside" (symbolized by our psychic and social life) are forever in a state of porous communication and cocreation. Working with dreams and other forms of emotional expressions, the richness of free association, the freedom to think beyond binaries and polarities, our work in classes is characterized by an enhanced appreciation of approaching life as it comes, of valuing chaos and ambiguity, and of becoming alive to one's subjective, interpersonal, and politico-historical context. In all of this, the attempt is to try to enhance dialogical currents by fostering a climate of empathetic and deep listening in the classroom. The task before us as a class is also of strengthening cooperative interpersonal currents even as we mindfully engage with the emerging themes from the course content.

Explorations in Experiential Pedagogy

While teaching psychology, psychotherapy and psychoanalysis, in some courses, I concentrate on immersive and experiential pedagogy. This pedagogical mode is never free of potential perils and difficulties. Nevertheless, it is indeed rich and has some transformative possibilities, if the upheavals that come one's way are acknowledged and made sense of jointly by the facilitator as well as the group. As an illustration, let me present a few moments from my work with students over the years. In these courses I generally approach the syllabus in a way that makes my students think of their self, immediate relationships, and revisiting broken connections. I also encourage them to examine their blind spots vis-à-vis the suffering of others who are disadvantaged due to socio-historical reasons. The self and the world are understood as being coterminous and continuous. Thinking beyond the anthropometric viewpoint is encouraged. The attempt is for students to rethink their relationship with all other living beings and forms in nature, including plants.

Crisis points in personal life are viewed as challenges that offer opportunities for ingathering, renewal and growth. The courses build on the value of insight through self-awareness. The self is understood as being non-cohesive, yet vast and rich, multilayered and multidimensional. Even as the importance of identifying forms of structural oppression and injustice in the outer world is highlighted, similar proclivities in the self towards violence and discrimination are meditated upon. The propensity to project blame and negativity to sources external to the self is gradually replaced by an introspective gaze. Perspective taking is encouraged. This enables a different imagination of political action, one which is not based exclusively on hate and rage, but one in which there is reparative action without necessarily inflicting fresh wounds on the body and mind of the collective. The crux of the teaching philosophy and pedagogy lies in reaching freedom in one's inner life and enhancing empathy—both for the self as well as for others (including the 'othered' within the self). Such a critical educational perspective is held in place by a pedagogical framework in which compassion and care are not enforced as superego ideals but are nurtured as potentials to be released when frozen states of anger, anxiety, bitterness and hurt are possibly worked through in the student's life.

As the classroom livens up through readings and discussions on chosen themes, at times the group too begins to offer itself as a holding environment wherein some students eventually come to find a fresh way of appreciating their past, their familial and social world. Disentangling from a cacophony of noises—parental and social injunctions as well as moralistic internalizations—they move to find their personal voice.

This process initiates a reexamination of relational spaces in their lives which may have been locked in impasses. To briefly share, let me pick up a few moments from courses such as Experiencing the Self: Relating Self to Others and Listening, Relating and Communicating, both of which are informed by a psychoanalytical and phenomenological perspective. Apprehending the articulations of the unconscious, in these courses, we approach the subject matter of self and Communication as a field which is full of desires and wishes, also ambivalences and contradictions (we also think of the secrets we keep and the lies which we tell ourselves and others and their intimate relationship with our subjective truths). The main objective of the courses is to help young people open themselves up in an experiential sense. In addition, the courses facilitate an appreciation of what in the self and in others cannot be listened to and engaged with, and thus, in turn presents itself as a state of anxiety or invokes restlessness, irritation, anger, rage, depression, and/or a wish to escape from situations, dissociate, foreclose communication, and so on and so forth.

Over the years, I have had students come back to tell me how they have started on a process of seeing their parents as persons and not reducing them to 'it' like entities- figures who are only there to fulfill certain functions in their life. Participation in these courses has made students appreciate the human condition of their parents, especially fathers, whom they may have written off for a long time. (In my observation, this is more frequently the case with sons than daughters). For a few, the image of an absent or distant, authoritarian or reckless, unfeeling father gives way to a man with his own limitations, anguish and vulnerabilities. Some students make their first attempts to receive their father differently, to thaw the ice after prolonged periods of non-communication with the latter.[1]

Others have before them the task of reworking their relationship with the mother, of finding a place for self beyond a fused enmeshment with the mother. The challenge here could be of remaining involved with the mother's life and her wishes and yet also having a center of one's personal existence. Still other students begin to inwardly receive and listen to lovers and friends differently. A few move to recover humanism and psychic meaning in intimate relationships which might have ended in bitterness a long while ago. For another subset of students, the struggle is to find their voice even as they feel oppressed by the weight of historical injustices meted out to the fabric of their collective selfhood. Being a woman, a Dalit, a refugee, a disabled person, a non-valued migrant, an economically disadvantaged person, the readings and discussion themes help them to reflect on their complex subject positions where the 'I' emerges in relation to the 'You' that had so far been seen only as an oppressor. In this realm there is much to self-reflexively think about the emerging 'I' and the 'You'. The burden of political violence and oppression is huge. Classroom processes, reading material and accompanying pedagogical approaches serve as an initial container for young people trying to relate anew with their emerging subject positions.[2]

1. The trends that I am indicating here with respect to mothers and fathers are the more usual ones. In no way do they exhaust the realm of feelings that students experience for their mothers or fathers. There are those who as sons and daughters feel immense closeness with their fathers. Others may have an intensely difficult relationship with the mother. As can be imagined, the field of human relations is complex indeed. For want of space I am only sharing the dominant aspects which have sometimes emerged subsequent to classroom processes.

2. It is crucial to mention here that similar and parallel processes would be initiated in other courses by colleagues. The opening up of the student's subjectivity in Psychology programmes at AUD should thus be recognized as the joint effort of several teachers. My teaching explorations are only a miniscule part of the entire team's effort.

Whatever be the issues that students are grappling with, in almost every instance, I have found there is some reflection to be undertaken, some forgiveness to be sought, and also some forgiving to be extended. Of course such classes can pose hugely trying and difficult challenges. There are moments where one is not able to facilitate the emotional flow successfully. There are times when instead of listening and sharing, there is chaos prevailing in the classroom.

At times, the group looks disinterested, bored, tired and unempathetic. These are real moments too. They have to be survived through by the facilitator and students. In my experience, a return to the earlier state of balance has usually been possible. We return to repair the ruptures and breaks in the dialogical process. As a group, we slowly realize that to open the self to observation and exploration, and to an acknowledgment of vulnerability, is an effort which is often fraught with many tensions but also some richness. Theoretically, the ethic in the classroom is one of receiving each one's experience, including the text which is being read, with respect and curiosity. In actuality, this may not always be the case and breaks from the group ethic become points for further introspection.

In my repeated experience, a large class in MA Psychology hinders a fuller containment and understanding of delicate feeling states. This has meant that experiential work has to be carefully balanced with readings, screening and discussion of films and the use of related educational material. In MPhil Psychoanalytic Psychotherapy and MPhil Development Practice, batches where the number of students is fewer, there is greater ease in experiential exploration. However, with any group of students, as the course facilitator, I remain preoccupied with how best to balance initiation into experience with related pedagogical tools and texts that have an evocative texture and quality. An immersive and experiential pedagogy also demands that there are adequate opportunities which provide for psychic closure as the course concludes. The students must move out of the semester with a feeling of safety and not with a sense of overwhelming vulnerability. The objective of self-directed courses is to initiate a long-term introspective and self-reflexive process in students without flooding them with feeling states that are too difficult to be managed once the classes conclude. This is crucial as in some instances, courses based on experiential pedagogy can infuse the classroom with far too much raw affect which can be experienced as trying (even traumatic) by the students. The facilitator is required to use pedagogy and course material in such a manner that a balance (even if an imperfect one) is reached between the unravelling of the subjective and its relationship to larger frames of shared reference so as to see one's distinctive individuality and the universality of human experience simultaneously, to feel one's pain and to relate it to that of others as well. A balancing between acknowledging pain and suffering and also considering the sources of gratitude, richness and joy in one's existence is of importance.

The teaching pedagogy and course material have to be interwoven thoughtfully. To establish the foundations of a critical-experiential pedagogy, I generally include readings from psychology and a number of interdisciplinary sources. We dwell on the subject matter through discussions, sessions of group sharing, reading literary short stories and novellas, watching films, sometimes even by listening to music, reading poems, viewing paintings and by focusing on the human psyche through autobiographical and biographical narrations. All of these retain the dual focus of attending to the personal and simultaneously, of extending the self via sympathetic imagination to a contextual appreciation of the other. The classroom ethic is of listening to and staying with differences without quickly converting them into polarities or hierarchies.

Introspective Realizations

A lesson I learnt early in my teaching explorations was to not become too attached to 'a particular (kind of) student' or a 'set of students', in spite of the pull being a real one in this direction. I realized that I needed to be attentive to various tunes and melodies in the class. An important challenge to guard against was of converting my students into narcissistic extensions of my own self. Have I been seeking an affirmation of my thoughts from them primarily for the sake of maintaining my own self esteem? I looked around at colleagues and realized that this propensity is widely present in many of us. It could considerably limit our role as a facilitator.

This also led me to consider the classroom as any other social and political site laced with differential histories of privilege and discrimination, and access or denial to resources. I asked myself the introspective question—what were the kinds of voices that I liked to hear in the classroom and which ones did I tend to put down? Who were the students who often spoke in my classes? Were there others who tended to remain silent and why? Did I make any special effort to evoke responses from the hesitant ones by creating special conditions of nurturance, tolerance and love for them to emerge forth? This made me think further about the particular set of subjective locations which framed my world view. They provided the mode through which I listened to and received my students in the classroom. I needed to be in greater touch with the responses I evoked in others and which in turn were evoked in me through classroom interactions. Some students challenged me and made me feel uncomfortable. How best did I survive their confrontation? I was ushered into a reflective process to think through whether the student was bringing up something that I was not ready to receive. In order to defend myself, did I tend to look at the student through a biased eye?

The above challenge has acquired renewed density with years of experience. As a supervisor of MPhil and doctoral students, and as a clinician training others through immersive years of painstaking work in psychotherapy, the levels of proximity in thoughts and feelings we share are enormous. And yet after a long process of cojourneying, when students became colleagues and tended to question back (at times with overt aggression) the notions we had acquired together, this twisted turn felt difficult to bear and survive. Survival here has been contingent on recovering an inner capacity to lovingly return again and again, to hold one's ideals in place, to contain differences between oneself and former students in a reflexive manner and to see that our joint work has a life and purpose beyond the present conflicts entangling the third space between us at any given moment in time. At times, love is not what one can 'ingather' within the self. A shadow of the surrounding darkness envelops it temporarily. In those times, what has helped is to realize that even if one cannot not succeed or survive the moment with grace, yet one is able to eventually return after acknowledging the despair. What also helped is the awareness that in spite of temporary conflicts, a return to our joint vision, purpose and imagination is still possible. By keeping alive an introspective gaze I have refocused on the joint possibilities before us. This entire process, however, has been far from easy and perhaps this is what at present surfaces as one of the greater challenge in my teaching career.

Education as a Site of Fear, Power and Control

Sometimes I have wondered over the hesitation and fear with which some students approach teachers even before they actually know a teacher's particular temperament. This has made me think of the fantasies about and experiences with teachers that they carry from school to college to university. The image of a teacher as a figure of authority gets consolidated for innumerable students in our society much before they reach the university level. It is no wonder then that as transference figures we are easily converted into symbols of authority, even if our particular temperaments encourage dialogue. I have considered this as an added dimension of my work as a university teacher.

The teaching process itself is a living site laced with power and its dynamics. Erik Erikson, the well-known psychoanalyst advises us that we think about power not alone from the angle of structural analysis but also from the dimension of infancy and early childhood. Erikson (1964) points in the direction that we all participate in inevitable hierarchies as infants and children. The manner in which power is handled by our parents in the first stage of life has a crucial bearing on how we use or abuse it in later stages of life. It raises an important concern here. Were we made to feel our smallness and vulnerability, and was it held and respected or violated and exposed and put to shame?

To Erikson's emphasis on understanding power though the parent-infant relationship, I wish to add a second dimension – the relational dyad between the adult teacher and the growing child. Schools, colleges and finally universities become real-life fields where teachers demonstrate the ways in which issues of power, structure and hierarchy are enlivened and negotiated. In effect, as a teacher, I realize, I am also a guardian of the society's youth and have been entrusted with tremendous power. Therefore, at times, I turn inwards to ask myself questions such as: am I aware of the power I hold? Do I inculcate in my students, the feelings of smallness or the confidence to authentically voice their questions and doubts? At other times I am aware that the classroom represents a social formation in which the multidimensional dynamism of power moves and oscillates between the teacher and the group(s) of students.

Let me pause here to also think of the divide that so often characterizes intellect which becomes akin to cognition and emotion which is seen as personal, soft, non-objective, less worthy and outside the space of learning. If teaching is a relational process, then, learning can no longer center around the acquisition of knowledge and skills of the profession but equally so, and perhaps more importantly, on the inculcation of ways of being and living life. I ask myself the question, what kind of knowledge do I facilitate in classes, and how will it help my students to become more humane with a critical and reflexive eye? If universities are sites of crucial interface where we learn our first few serious lessons about the kind of civil society we want to create and participate in, then our classrooms can become the practice spaces of imagining, dreaming and fantasying about society in more emancipatory ways.

I wish to share a pedagogical issue here—psychoanalysis, a discipline in which I am trained, has a unique take on studenthood. Like in medicine, psychoanalytic students too aspire to become clinicians, involved in psychological healing. The distinctive part of training to become a psychoanalyst is that the future professional has to go through a prolonged process of self-work, where one becomes one's first patient. Howsoever brilliant a candidate may be intellectually, yet to train as a clinician she has to first and foremost observe and insightfully engage with her own internal processes and subject oneself to become a voluntary 'patient' in 'treatment' with a senior analyst. This training process takes years of rigorous work on the self and only subsequently does one become capable of working with the psychic distress and suffering of others. In my opinion, such a route to training that takes us towards 'objectivity' via an immersive plunge into our subjective processes has much to contribute to issues related to pedagogy in various social science disciplines. It imbues us with the value of mutual resonance (as the healer and sufferer are first and foremost equals- both are patients afflicted by life's sufferings) as well as of uncertainty and the space for creative self-doubt. It also helps in honing the self to become an instrument that vibrates in resonance with the other.

The more a teacher defends or denies her vulnerabilities and insecurities, the greater will be her need to exercise control and power in classroom. Instead if she is in touch with a range of feelings that belong to her personal life, she will tend to be more accepting and open to receiving the intellectual-emotional world of her students. To foster an empathetic climate in the classroom, a teacher needs to work with herself, and keep at 'becoming' human, ever in touch with the flows and blocks of her emotional life. This will enable her to remain flexible and less rigid, more accepting and less rejecting vis-à-vis her students. Herein lies the birth of a relational ethic based on equality and mutuality, infusing waves of vitality into the teaching-learning situation.

Being a Teacher Today

How can I close this essay without sharing a few worries that preoccupy me most acutely today? After teaching for almost twenty-four years, of late, I have had to reinvent ways of talking about politics and compassion in the same breath. This makes me wonder about the difficult shifts in the surrounding social climate. Are there ways in which we can think about and envision a form of politics which is based on love and not necessarily on anger, hate and retributive justice? This is a question that often accompanies my ruminations. Moreover, as identity struggles are becoming sharper in the present milieu, their impact on the teacher-student bond is also being registered. For all their positive sides, identity- based processes seem to carry the potential of sometimes dividing teachers and students into opposing identities—students vs. teachers, or teachers vs. students. Another challenge staring us in the face today is of institutes of higher education becoming akin to private industries which maximize the profit gained through student fees. The weight and demands of the market are heavy from all sides. The introduction of a high-fee model is definitely impacting the relationship between students and teachers. For all of the above and several other reasons, how will a critical, experiential and empathetic approach to teaching survive when the defining equation of the teacher and students is likely to shift from it being a relationship based on mutuality to that of an exchange between a client and a professional or a consumer and provider? Who will I be to my students and who will they be to me? My mind muddles in confusion as I mull over these questions which do not have any easy answer save a desire to preserve the dignity of this special bond.

In spite of the surrounding social chaos, let me end by sharing that during some of the deepest moments of personal despair and losses, I have been held and taken care of by my students. Reinstating faith and hope is also the realization that till today the classroom remains one of the few 'sacred' spaces of enrichment and learning for both students as well as teachers. It is here that teachers and students touch each other deeply. The beauty of this relationship imparts meaning and dignity to my life, just as it does for so many of my colleagues all across the world.

References

Erikson, E.H. (1964). *Insight and Responsibility*. New York: Norton.

Winnicott, D.W. (1958). *The Maturational Processes and the Facilitating Environment*. New York: International Universities Press.

List of Contributors

Richa Awasthy is currently working as Associate Professor in School of Business, Public Policy and Social Entrepreneurship at Ambedkar University Delhi (AUD). Before joining AUD she had worked with IMI, Delhi. She has an experience of more than twenty years in research, consultancy and teaching. She has published papers in reputed Indian and international journals. She is co-editor of *Qualitative Research in Management: Methods and Experiences.* She has presented papers in reputed national and international conferences, such as Academy of Management. Her current interests are cross-cultural studies, intercultural relations, organizational culture, organizational diagnosis, organizational learning and organizational change. She can be reached at richa@aud.ac.in

Suchitra Balasubrahmanyan teaches at the School of Design, Ambedkar University Delhi. Her research interests centre on nineteenth and twentieth-century craft and design in the Indian subcontinent from historical and sociological perspectives. She is author of "Craft and Design in the Hindu Way of Life" in *Encyclopaedia of Asian Design,* Vol. 4 (Bloomsbury Academic 2018), "Design in India" in *Bloomsbury Encyclopaedia of Design,* Vol. 2 (Bloomsbury Academic 2016); co-editor of *Atoot Dor/ Unbroken Thread: Banarasi Brocade Saris at Home and in the World* (National Museum 2016) and *Ahmedabad 600: Portraits of City* (Marg 2011); co-author of *Ahmedabad: From Royal City to Megacity* (Penguin 2011) and *The Shaping of Modern Gujarat:*

Plurality, Hindutva and Beyond (Penguin India 2005). She can be contacted at suchitra@aud.ac.in

Jatin Bhatt is a 1977 Industrial Design graduate with over forty years of combined experience of practice and academics. Reluctantly put into academic leadership to imagine and lead new programmes, he has focused on developing a vibrant and holistic ecology for learning. He believes that practice of knowledge needs to be understood not only as a condition to respond but more importantly, a challenge to transform it for the better. Curricula design and its transaction, empathy and compassion, enabling feedback and real-world network is as critical as reflective; the need is to bring together a motivated and cohesive faculty team with shared values and objectives. He is currently the Pro Vice Chancellor of the Ambedkar University Delhi (AUD) which he joined in 2012 as Professor and founding Dean of the School of Design. He can be reached at jatin@aud.ac.in

Sugandha Gupta worked at the Centre of Psychotherapy and Clinical Research, Ambedkar University Delhi, as a Consultant Psychiatrist from September 2015 till June 2018. She is the founder Director of Delhi Mind Clinic. An alumni of Sir Ganga Ram Hospital, she taught Psychiatry to undergraduate and postgraduate medical students, nursing students and clinical psychology students at Army College of Medical Sciences, Delhi, for three years. A staunch believer in bio-psycho-social model of mental illness, she strives to adopt a holistic approach towards her patients. Her clinical areas of interest are Cognitive Behavior Therapy, Brief Psychodynamic Psychotherapy and evidence based psychopharmacology. Besides this, she is an avid reader and a keen music lover. She may be reached at drsugandhagupta@gmail.com.

Anita Ghai joined as Professor of Disability Studies at the School of Human Studies, Ambedkar University Delhi in 2015. Before this, Anita Ghai was Associate Professor in the Department of Psychology, Jesus and Mary College, University of Delhi. Her areas of interest are Disability Studies, issues related to sexuality, psychology and gender. She can be contacted at anita@aud.ac.in

Shifa Haq, PhD, is a psychoanalytic psychotherapist and an Assistant Professor in Psychology-Psychotherapy, School of Human Studies, Ambedkar University Delhi. She is interested in studying gender, violence and mourning. She is currently undertaking an ongoing study on mourning and inter-generational trauma in the context of disappearance and militarization in Kashmir. She can be reached at shifahaq@aud.ac.in

Rachana Johri is Professor of Psychology at the School of Human Studies, Ambedkar University Delhi. Prior to this she taught Psychology at Lady Shri Ram College for Women, University of Delhi. At Ambedkar University Delhi, she has been involved in teaching and guiding research in psychosocial studies, gender studies, disability studies, mental health and psychotherapy. Much of her writing and research focuses on these intersections. However, the question of maternal subjectivity has been an abiding interest. As a teacher, she enjoys bringing diverse areas into the classroom, encouraging students to shed disciplinary boundaries and find connections between their personal biographies and academic interests. She can be reached at rachana@aud.ac.in

Mamatha Karollil has a PhD in Social Sciences (Psychology and Sociology) from the Tata Institute of Social Sciences. She teaches at the School of Human Studies in Ambedkar University Delhi. Her interests and commitments include feminism, psychoanalysis, queer politics, pedagogy, stories (as methodology and outside academy, sustenance), sex and sexuality, intimacies and community. She can be contacted at mamatha@aud.ac.in

Kuriakose Mamkoottam is Professor Emeritus of Business, Public Policy and Social Entrepreneurship at Ambedkar

University Delhi (AUD), and Executive Chairperson, AUD Centre for Incubation, Innovation & Entrepreneurship (ACIIE). He was the founding Director, School of Business, Public Policy and Social Entrepreneurship, and Dean, Student Services, at AUD during 2011-2016. Earlier, he was the Head and Dean, Faculty of Management Studies (FMS), University of Delhi, where he was Professor of Human Resource Management and Industrial Relations during 1985-2011. Professor Mamkoottam's academic interest incudes Human Resource Management, Industrial Relations, Technological Change, and Institution Building. He can be contacted at kurias@gmail.com

Shyam B. Menon teaches at the Central Institute of Education, University of Delhi. He has for years worked closely and intensely with teachers of schools and universities studying and working towards reforms in teaching and other institutional processes. His research interests are in Curriculum Studies, Higher Education and Teacher Education. He was Vice Chancellor of the Ambedkar University Delhi during its first ten years. He can be reached at shyambmenon@gmail.com

Krishna Menon works at the School of Human Studies, Ambedkar University Delhi. She is currently the Dean of the School and Professor of Gender Studies. Prior to joining Ambedkar University Delhi, she had taught for several years at Lady Shri Ram College, University of Delhi. She has a PhD in Political Science and is interested in feminist politics and questions of pedagogy as well as the performing arts. She can be reached at krishnamenon@aud.ac.in

Usha Mudiganti is an Assistant Professor in the School of Letters at Ambedkar University Delhi. She teaches courses on literatures in India, American literature and British literature. Her research interests include gender studies with specific focus on India, the constructions of childhoods in literature, childhood in post-colonial literature and the changing norms of childhood in a globalised world. She uses popular culture and critical theories such as psychoanalytic theory, close reading of texts, post-colonialism and feminism to debunk popular myths about gender and childhood. She can be contacted at usha@aud.ac.in

Shivani Nag is an Assistant Professor in the School of Education Studies, Ambedkar University Delhi. She has done her MPhil and PhD from Jawaharlal Nehru University, Delhi. Her PhD research focused on socio-cultural and linguistic inclusion of children in school education. She has taught courses in Departments of Psychology and Education Studies with focus on child development, learning theories and research methods. Her research interests include critical and feminist pedagogies, multilingual education and socio-cultural theories of learning and cognition. She can be contacted at shivani@aud.ac.in

Ashok Nagpal is Professor of Psychology at the School of Human Studies (SHS), Ambedkar University Delhi. He has been actively associated with the dissemination of psychoanalytic psychotherapy and cultural psychology for the last thirty five years in India. A psychoanalytic psychotherapist based in Delhi, he has been the first Director of Centre of Psychoanalytic Studies in Delhi University in 2006. Subsequently he shifted to AUD to establish the first of their kind Psychology programs in entire Asia drawing upon Psychosocial Clinical perspective as initiated in Erik Erikson's conceptions. He has been the Dean of School of Human Studies as well as Dean Academic Services, also Director, Centre of Psychotherapy and Clinical Research in AUD. He has published few essays, a notable one being "Freud: The Relational Yogi". He can be contacted at ashonag@aud.ac.in

Monishita Hajra Pande is Assistant Professor, Centre for English Language Education (CELE) in Ambedkar University Delhi (AUD). She teaches courses in English proficiency, linguistics and language teaching. She is also involved in teacher training projects. Her research interests include English language teacher education, cross-linguistic transfer of skills, multilingualism, peer mentoring and teacher and learner autonomy. She can be reached at monishita@aud.ac.in

Ashis Roy is a faculty member and psychoanalytic therapist at the Centre of Psychotherapy and Clinical Research, Ambedkar University Delhi. He is especially interested in working with states of mental fragmentation and processes characterized by 'negation' in the lives of his patients. His doctoral work is in the area of the construction of the self and the other in intimate Hindu-Muslim relationships in India. Ashis Roy has been teaching psychology, psychoanalysis and has been a practicing psychotherapist since 2009. While creating a frame of clinical research in India, where narratives emanating from psychotherapy are the central focus, he has supervised research works of post-graduate students in the field of suicide, psychosis, and other areas,. He is currently a training candidate with Indian Psychoanalytic Society, Kolkata, a unit of IPA. He can be reached at ashis@aud.ac.in

Vinod R. is a teacher at School of Human Studies (SHS), Ambedkar University Delhi. He also offers papers at School of Education Studies (SES). Some of the courses he teaches at AUD are: Experiencing the Self; Listening, Communicating and Relating; Understanding Childhood; Experiencing Education: Immersed Reflections; and Psychosocial Experience of Educational Failure. Before joining AUD in 2010, he taught at the Central Institute of Education (University of Delhi) and Lady Shri Ram College for Women for eight years. His academic interests are in the areas of listening and pedagogy; poverty and psychoanalysis; interdisciplinary linkages between psychoanalysis and education. He is also trying to evolve and situate linkages between autoethnobiography and experiential pedagogy as a research method; and works on the ideal of becoming and being a barefoot group psychologist. He can be reached at vinod@aud.ac.in

Deepti Sachdev is an Assistant Professor at the School of Human Studies, Ambedkar University Delhi. She is deeply interested in psychoanalysis as a mode of unconscious knowledge and healing. Committed to working with the disadvantaged, she dreams of the ways in which analytic work and insights can be brought closer to the lives of the urban poor. She values pedagogic forms that create classrooms as safe and enlivening spaces for group work and for articulating the hitherto silenced voices. She enjoys writing poetry, doodling, eating chocolates and tending to her plants. She can be reached at deepti@aud.ac.in

Vatsala Saxena has her PhD in Psychology from the University of Delhi. Presently, she is Assistant Professor of Psychology at the School of Human Studies, Ambedkar University Delhi. Her research interests lie in the areas of childhood/family and social psychology. She can be reached at vatsala@aud.ac.in

Devika Sharma is currently pursuing her PhD from Jamia Millia Islamia. She taught for some years at Ambedkar University Delhi. Before joining the university she had also taught as a primary teacher in a school. She can be reached at devikavangogh@gmail.com.

Gunjan Sharma is Assistant Professor at the School of Education Studies, Ambedkar University Delhi. Her professional focus is on education studies and education policy-politics, particularly at school and teacher education levels. She has worked with various government and non-government organisations on matters of education policy and has served in various capacities on the national level teacher education policy framing process in India. Gunjan Sharma has a doctoral degree in the area of sociology of education from the University of Delhi. During 2016-17, she completed her Fulbright-Nehru Postdoctoral research on the policy implications of publication networks in teacher education. She can be reached at gunjan@aud.ac.in

Anirban Sengupta is an Assistant Professor at the School of Development Studies, Ambedkar University Delhi. His area of research includes entrepreneurship-society interrelationship, interaction between state policies and entrepreneurship, private investment in higher education, and questions around research methodology. He is the author of *Entrepreneurship and Social Capital: Relationships and Start-ups in Indian ICT Industry*. Articles written by him have been published in edited books and different journals including *Sociological Bulletin, Journal of Entrepreneurship* and *International Journal of Educational Development*. He has also been engaging with the outcome of privatization of school education and writing about the same in popular media. He can be reached at anirban@aud.ac.in

Amit Singh teaches English at Ambedkar University Delhi. His areas of interest comprise folklore, oral traditions, spatiality, and epics. He is also interested in world literatures, diaspora studies, marginal literatures, and theory and criticism. He offers courses based on these areas at undergraduate and graduate levels. Currently, he is engaged in investigating the folkloric traditions surrounding the *Kumbh Mela* at Prayag. He can be reached at amit@aud.ac.in

Vijaya Shankar Varma has a PhD in Theoretical Physics from Imperial College and he has taught at the Department of Physics and Astrophysics of the University of Delhi. He has been Director of the Computer Centre, of the Centre for Science Education and Communication and Dean Planning. After retirement he was Advisor Planning at Ambedkar University Delhi and a National Fellow of the Indian Institute of Advanced Study, Shimla. For his work in school science education he was awarded The World Academy of Science Regional Prize. He is Distinguished Professor of the Philosophy of Science at Ambedkar University Delhi. He can be reached at varma2@gmail.com

Diamond Oberoi Vahali is Associate Professor of Literature in the School of Letters, Ambedkar University Delhi. She has co-edited and co-authored *Once Upon a Time: A Collection of Short Stories* and *Life and Times of Shanta Toofani: Story of a Survivor*. She has published articles pertaining to literature and cinema and is mainly interested in Indian Literature, Cinema Studies, Psychoanalysis, Life Writing and Memory Studies, Folklore, Indigenous Studies, Orature and in pursuing research in documenting films and narratives that have dealt with people's struggles. She can be contacted at diamond@aud.ac.in

Honey Oberoi Vahali teaches at the School of Human Studies, AUD. She is a psychoanalyst, and a clinical psychologist. She is interested in forging bridges between psychoanalysis, streams of compassion and visions of social justice. It has been her endeavour to conceptualize a model of psychotherapy in Indian context that responds to lived experiences of social as well as emotional suffering. She is the founding Director of the Centre of Psychotherapy and Clinical Research, AUD. Teaching for her is most of all a relational encounter, a process that can potentially transform the being of the teacher as well as of her students. Her book *Lives in Exile: Exploring the Inner World of Tibetan Refugees* (2009, Routledge) is an exposition detailing the on-going struggle of three generations of Tibetans in exile. She can be reached at honey@aud.ac.in

